# Layoff Proof Your Job

## Cracking the Layoff Code

J. Barry Wood

ISBN: 1-4392-3854-5
ISBN-13: 9781439238547

To order additional copies, please contact us.
BookSurge
www.booksurge.com
1-866-308-6235
orders@booksurge.com

dedication: **To The Americans Who Have Lost Their Jobs**

*Layoff Proof Your Job* is dedicated to the millions of American working, career, and professional men and women who have made our country strong. Your sacrifice and superior work-ethic have made our country great. Millions of you have experienced layoffs, closings, and outsourcings. Many of you have not only lost your jobs, you have lost your houses as well.

You have not lost your dignity, your pride, your courage, your hope, and your faith in God. Your resiliency, tenacity, and longing for a better tomorrow inspire hope for a better future for our families and our nation. Hold your heads up high, you are among the people who have made America the great nation she is, and you will live to work another day.

# Table of Contents

Introduction                                                          ix

1. Breaking Out Of the Cookie-Cutter Mold                              1

2. Cracking the Layoff Code                                            5
3. A Snapshot of Layoffs in America                                   17
4. Layoff Proof Your Job                                              21

5. Job-Saving Steps You Can Take                                      69
6. From Hope to Hopelessness and Back Again                           75
7. Warning Signs That Predict Layoffs                                 83

8. Getting the Raise or Promotion You Deserve                         97
9. Learn from Life's Winners, Not Life's Whiners                     123
10. There Is Life After Layoff                                       127

introduction: You are relaxing, deeply immersed in your favorite book, when your doorbell rings. Though you were not expecting anyone, you are not surprised when you open the door to find your friend from down the street. Detecting the quizzical look on your face, he puts you at ease by saying that nothing is wrong, that he wants only five minutes of your time. He is a trusted friend, so you invite him in.

A stock broker by trade, he begins telling you about a new company that is ready with its initial public stock offering. He tells you that this opportunity, if acted upon, is guaranteed to make you some money. Having heard stories about people who lost a lot of money in the stock market, you are very skeptical. But, since he is your friend, you agree to listen. So convincing is his story, you decide to write him a check for $1,000, and ask him to get you in on the ground floor of this investment opportunity. As you watch him walk down your driveway, you stand there hoping that you have not made the wrong decision.

During the next few months you witness phenomenal growth in the stock your neighbor talked you into buying. Your initial $1,000 investment grows to $5,000 and then to $10,000. Each pay period finds you buying a few more shares of stock. Suddenly, you realize that you have become very interested in investing and the stock market. You enjoy watching your portfo-lio grow as you begin building yourself a fortune. Each time you see your friend you thank him for including you in this invest-ment gold mine.

The story illustrates the point that sometimes you need to act upon a tip which can make a major difference in the lives of both you and your family. This prin-ciple is true when it comes to layoff proof-ing your job.

I contend that there are certain clearly-defined steps you may take that can help you layoff proof your job. I also believe that the most effective strategy available for layoff proofing your job is to layoff proof yourself.

The following is written with the con-viction that honesty and truth are what most readers expect.

# Chapter 1
# Breaking Out Of the Cookie-Cutter Mold

Have you ever awakened to the wonderful scent of gingerbread cookies fresh from the oven? My wife and daughter always bake gingerbread cookies at Christmas. The heavenly smell of those warm cookies coming out of the oven is an experience everyone in our house enjoys. I can smell them now. The very first time they baked cookies together was one of those cute YouTube moments we will never forget. There stood our daughter, spatula in hand, a bit of cookie dough on her cheek, perched on a stool, swallowed up in an apron, and up to her elbows in flour. "Little Miss Independent" temporarily took charge of the kitchen. My wife guided her as she measured the flour, sugar, vanilla, and ginger into the mixing bowl and added the butter and eggs. Together, they mixed and rolled the dough. Next came her favorite part as she took the cookie cutter in her tiny hand and stamped out a dozen cookies. She squealed with joy, knowing that she had transformed that flat sheet of dough into little gingerbread men. They placed them on a cookie sheet, popped them into the oven, and voila, out came toasty brown gingerbread men. Amazed at how uniform the cookies were, my seven-year-old daughter said: "Mommy, they are all the same." Oh, the wisdom that comes from the mouths of babes.

Have you ever felt like a cookie-cutter employee in a layoff driven world? It seems that everyone acts, looks, works, and performs just like everybody else. Unfortunately, most of the people where you work are satisfied with the status quo. They plan to sit tight, not rock the boat, work the same way they have always worked, and hope that they don't get laid off.

You probably already know it...your fellow employees have just handed you a tremendous advantage. This can be a golden opportunity if you are willing to break out of the cookie-cutter mold. You can use their indifference, lack of motivation, and poor performance to your advantage.

This is where you can begin making yourself layoff proof. The power to break out of the cookie-cutter mold lies within you. How do you break out of the mold? That is what the rest of this book is about, but here are a few hints. In the following chapters you will learn how to:
- Break out of the cookie-cutter mold
- Layoff proof yourself and your job
- Rocket to the top 10% of your company
- Positively impact your boss
- Distinguish yourself from others where you work
- Discover the secrets of your boss's private layoff list
- Spot an impending layoff before it takes place
- Become an employee to be kept at all costs
- Develop plans that will enable you to succeed
- Muster the courage to dare to be different
- Learn to position yourself for a raise or promotion
- Know when to ask and when not to ask for a raise or promotion

What kind of positive impact would you have on your job if you were to suddenly break out of the mold of being just like everyone else? To say the least, your boss would be impressed. In fact, he might be so impressed that he keeps you employed at all costs. In the pages ahead, you will discover that there are many things you can do to enable you to become one of the top employees in your company. Relax; take a week or a weekend to analyze your job, your company, your boss, and to develop your personalized game plan. Choose to focus your energies on the things you can do to make a difference for yourself, your career, and your company.

By the time you finish reading this book you will know how to layoff proof yourself and your job. In addition, you will never again be satisfied just to be another cookie-cutter employee.

To better understand how bosses make up their minds when they consider who they will lay off, join me in examining layoffs from a business owner's perspective.

# Chapter 2
# Cracking the Layoff Code

---

*Layoff Proof Your Job* was written to provide you with advantages. These advantages include several things. As you learn to layoff proof yourself and your job, the first advantage you will gain is that of learning how to crack the layoff code where you are employed. What is a layoff code anyway? It is a set of guidelines used by either a boss or a company to decide which employees to retain and which ones to lay off. Think of your company's layoff code as a template. When a company begins laying people off, its layoff code is what it uses to determine which employees will be laid off.

Your first goal in layoff proofing yourself will be that of cracking the layoff code your boss or company might use. Once you discover the criteria they would use to begin layoffs, you can make certain that you don't fit their layoff template. The first step in this process will be getting into your boss's mind to understand layoffs from his or her perspective. After that, you will discover how to develop a personal strategy that will equip you with both the knowledge and the ability to make yourself layoff proof. Don't worry, you will know how to develop your own personal plan of action by the time you finish this book.

Advantages are not accidental; they are planned. For you to become layoff proof, you will need to implement your own personal plan. It will be much easier than you think. If you are willing to discover certain principles of success and make any necessary changes to your work-ethic, you will be rewarded. The good news is that you will be rewarded handsomely. Your rewards will be many, including using your advantages over most of the other employees where you work. Also, you will become a significantly stronger employee who is in most circumstances, layoff proof. The bad news is that due to the depressed economy, some will experience layoffs no matter what they do or how well they perform. The truth is that many companies will be forced to downsize or cease to exist. It is the nature of the beast.

Gaining an advantage over other employees who work for your company will be much easier than you think. Why? Because most of your fellow employees either lack the knowledge to take the necessary steps to layoff proof themselves, they are too lazy to do so, or they sense that there are steps they need to take but are unwilling to take them. Your advantage comes when you discover which steps to take, and boldly take them.

Let's begin by discovering the first of the major advantages you can achieve by beginning to crack the layoff code. Understanding this code will enable you to gain an accurate understanding of how your boss or business owner understands and approaches layoffs. Once you have discovered this secret, you can then position yourself to be included in the group that remains employed after a layoff is implemented.

### Getting Into Your Boss's Mind to Understand Layoffs

If only you could understand your boss's perspective concerning layoffs. The key question is this: "What motivates your boss to select some employees for layoffs, some to continue working, and a few to be fired?" How much would it be worth to you to gain this understanding? The answer to this question might be worth a sack of gold, for if you knew the answer to this question you would be able to layoff proof your job.

If you want to know the answer to that question, your best strategy is to ask your boss. Depending on the relationship you have with your boss and the level of job security you enjoy, the best way to discover what he or she thinks about layoffs is to ask them. If they are willing to tell you their approach to layoffs you can develop an effective game-plan to keep your job. If you do not have the type of relationship that would allow you to ask them, or your job situation is already tenuous at best, that's alright. For now, you may decide against asking them anything about layoffs. You may decide it best not to jeopardize your job by asking. The last thing you need to do is to target yourself for a lay-off. Don't be discouraged and don't give up. All is not lost; I will be introducing another strategy in the pages ahead. For now, be open to discovering new ways to begin developing your own goals and plans to make you a stronger employee and to layoff proof yourself. You can do it and, believe me, it is not that difficult.

I have worked for bosses, I have been a boss, and I have known many other bosses. The following is a composite of many of the insights I have gained into the way bosses think and make decisions. It should give you another perspective of your boss's way of thinking. Let's begin cracking the layoff code that hardly anyone knows exists.

## If you Were in Charge of Layoffs, What Would You Do?

In order to gain an understanding of the layoff process from your boss's perspective, pretend for a few moments that you are a business owner. Imagine that you started your own company 12 years ago. Today, you manage it and oversee its day-to-day operations. Both you and your company have been financially successful and have exhibited impressive growth. Through numerous struggles, personal sacrifices, great risks, and long hours, you built your business from three employees to its present level of 117. Your company, Airex, has been your personal success story. Its annual economic impact upon your town equals $11 million. The town where your business is located is dependent upon both the jobs it provides and the goods and services it supplies.

This year, orders are down and the recession has reduced your annual economic impact to $7 million. Profits have fallen precipitously while expenses have increased exponentially. As owner, you are forced to come to a devastating, but inescapable conclusion. Jobs must be cut, and they must be cut now. This is reality, not a business seminar exercise. Over the past few months you have directed the company's efforts to cut costs dramatically. Like almost everything else you attempt, your efforts have been very successful. However, there is still significant paring that must be done.

Airex faces closure unless you are able to significantly reduce your payroll. You never thought this day would come. In fact, if someone had approached you two years ago and said that you would soon be overseeing a layoff you would have told them that they were crazy. Now, the economy has brought you to the point where you are forced to lay off 20 employees in order for your company to survive. Survival...until now, that word was never in your vocabulary. You still find it impossible to believe.

The dreaded day of reckoning has arrived. You block off your appointment calendar, enter your office, shut the door, and tell your administrative assistant that you are not to be disturbed for any reason. You pray for the Lord to guide you as you make the tough decisions that lie ahead. You glance at your watch; it is 3:00 PM. By six, you plan to be finished and join your daughter for dinner at her favorite restaurant. Frustration sets in, an hour has gone by and you realize that you have accomplished absolutely nothing. The seriousness of what you are doing has sunk in and you realize that this is going to be one of the toughest things you have ever had to do. Staring you in the face is a blank yellow legal pad. You are reminded of your commitment not to leave work until you have selected the names of 20 people to include on your layoff list.

Where do you begin? You start with the newest hires and quickly determine that fairness dictates those five have to go. That leaves you with 15 slots to fill. But, these are not just slots to fill. Those 15 lines represent 15 people whose families are about to experience the shock of their lives. Attempts to write draw nothing but blanks as you are unable to produce any more names. Next, you decide to review lists of workers from various departments. Consideration is given to departments that are excelling and those that have declined. Again, no new names are written on your legal pad. This process is much more difficult than you ever imagined it could be. You call your daughter and apologize in advance for breaking your date. She knew that you planned to complete your list today. You tell her what a difficult time you are having, and she assures you that you have a raincheck for a night next week.

As you hang up the phone, the first question you ask yourself is this: "Who can Airex do without?" A few people come to mind and you write their names on your legal pad. Next, you realize that this would be a good time to remove certain employees who are non-productive. You add two more names to your list. Now, you feel that you are getting somewhere.

Suddenly, you smell roses. You look at your watch...7 PM. Your mind turns to the beautiful and fragrant rose garden your spouse and you enjoy. For a moment, it seems that you can actually smell the roses. But you can't, you realize that you didn't smell roses at all, it was a memory. Tonight, you feel as though you are involved in a dreaded process of "pruning." The stakes are high. Airex's very survival depends upon these layoffs.

Your mind snaps back to the most unpleasant task-at-hand. The words "company survival," pop in your mind. But people's families and future careers are at stake. Which people will be laid off? You realize that nothing in your background has prepared you for this. Selecting 20 people's names is the hardest decision you have ever had to make. "Playing with people's lives," you say, "I'm not God; I'm not qualified to make these decisions. If only God would drop a note on my desk with the 20 names already written out my struggle would be over." Then he reminds you that the struggle is an important part of your decision-making process. You thank him for his leadership and reflect on how it is so emotionally devastating to know that you are playing with people's lives. Many of your employees are friends. Some of them have worked for you for 10 years. Now, some of them will have to go. This day has been one that you feared might come. For months, you have had this nagging feeling deep inside, that it might come to this. It is gut-wrenching. You feel sick to your stomach. These are people who have sacrificed for you. They helped make your company what it is today. They are people you know intimately. Some of them stood by your side as you grieved over losing your father. You are deciding to lay off people who have families and young children, the same children you saw at the hospital when they were born. You and your spouse also attended some of your employee's weddings. Now their lives will be changed forever. These are families with mortgage payments, health issues, car payments, and family problems. Some may lose their houses. Some may even lose their marriages. Some may never recover. One of the last things you wish to do is to exacerbate any of their problems.

Blame sets in. You begin asking yourself: "What could I have done differently?" No rational answers are available. For a moment you struggle with the fleeting thought of laying off no one. It would be so much easier to maintain status quo. You allow your mind to drift back to the better days when things were booming. Suddenly, the stark reality of your company's possible closure calls you back to the task before you. The blame-game continues: "It is entirely my fault. No, it is not all my fault at all; I have done everything humanly possible to keep this company from tanking. The blame rests squarely upon the shoulders of Presidents Bush and Obama, and the madly out-of-control spending of the United States Congress." Finally you decide that there is enough blame to go around for everyone to have their share of culpability. You decide that the blame game is a dead end issue and begin searching for a solution to your problems.

To think that 96 other employees' jobs and their families' financial security may depend upon what you do in your office tonight is beyond sobering. You feel like a criminal. It is as though you are acting as the financial judge, jury, and executioner over the lives of 20 families. The only way you can force yourself to proceed is to remind yourself again that it is not only Airex's survival that is in question. Unless you make these tough decisions now, the remaining 96 employees will all lose their jobs when Airex closes three or four months from now. Though it is painful, that thought forces you to move on. You have 18 names on your legal pad.

Knowing that you will be blasted with unjust criticism because of your decision to lay people off is depressing. If the news media only had a clue of the struggle you are experiencing, they would never utter a single criticism. At this point, what people say about you is the least of your worries. You are startled and jump out of your chair when the phone rings. Who could be calling at 9 PM? It's your spouse...you offer an apology. Will this night ever end? You have been at it for six hours, and you are still not finished. You chastise yourself, for you have always prided yourself in being decisive, instinctive, and an insightful leader. Now you feel as though you are nothing more than a jellyfish. Dealing with these upcoming layoffs is taking its toll on your emotions. You can't bear to inflict this much pain into your employees' lives.

If only they knew. You don't dare tell them that over the past three months you have plowed most of your life-savings back into your company to help keep it afloat. Your actions probably spared many employees' jobs for a few extra weeks. You want no glory and you are not a martyr; you decide that they must never know.

Knowing that you must finalize your list you now turn your attention to employees that have not lived up to their potential and show no promise of doing so. Their names are included. Your attention turns to employees who have either demonstrated consistently bad attitudes or who have proven that they are not team-players. You write down two more names. Finally, you consider employees who are consistently late, absent, cause problems, and are generally undependable. As you finish your list you add a few additional names. They are those who have distinguished themselves as being purely negative people as well as the name of one known troublemaker.

It is 10 PM and you are finally finished. You review your list one last time. It contains 26 people's names. The goal of 20 people was reached and you have six alternates. You go home, read a while, go to bed at 2 AM, and endure a sleepless night.

The next morning, you meet with two department managers and your Human Resources manager to review your list and receive their input. One manager is absent. He was not invited since you decided that he will be terminated.

You and your managers begin the process of evaluating the people on your layoff list. One by one each name is discussed. The merits of their work, attitude, initiative, drive, cooperativeness, and their overall value to the company determine their status. Your managers persuade you that three of the original 20 should be retained because they had more information about their work than you. Those three whom you allowed to stay were replaced by three people from among your list of alternates. As the meeting ends, you have a final list of 20 people's names that will be laid off. Your assistant manager will be number 21. The layoffs will be implemented tomorrow.

The process was painful because everyone involved knew of the dramatic impact these decisions would have upon people's lives. The meeting is adjourned as you admonish your managers not to discuss any of this information with anyone. Now that the decisions have been finalized, you instruct your HR manager to begin preparing layoff notices and to make the necessary arrangements for severance checks, unemployment information, COBRA health insurance options, and pertinent 401(k) information.

Friday arrives and you have already set the schedule for delivery of the 21 layoff notices. Your strategy is for your HR and other managers to join you in meeting with the 20 employees individually. At that time you will give each person their layoff notice, hand them their severance check, and explain the process of applying for unemployment and other benefits. You will terminate your assistant manager at the end of the process.

By the end of the day, 20 employees', and one manager's lives have changed drastically. As they leave work, they do not have jobs. The layoffs have taken a heavy emotional toll upon you, your managers, and all remaining employees as well. Dealing with the pain on people's faces and the panic in their voices was emotionally draining for each of you. It is an experience that you hope you will never have to face again.

Employee morale has plummeted. Many fear that they will be the next person summoned to your office to receive their layoff notice. To allay their fears, you call everyone together and explain that the layoffs were mandatory. You explain that they were implemented because of the terrible state of the economy and that there were simply no other options at this time. To offer some much-needed reassurance, you tell everyone that no additional layoffs are planned, and everyone who was not laid off today still has their job. In an attempt to put your best spin on the situation, you challenge the remaining employees to pick up the slack and close the gaps left by the 21 who just lost their jobs.

The meeting is over. Most of your employees leave work in a bittersweet mood. They are happy to still have their jobs and most are empathetic toward the 21 who lost theirs. You believe the company can survive, but right at this moment, you feel the weight of the world upon your shoulders. Those 21 families stay on your mind.

**Reflection**

As you finished the story, how do you feel about the way the owner handled the situation? What would you have done differently? Spend a few moments thinking about how you would have approached that situation had you been owner of the Airex Company.

**Put it All Together**

Perhaps you gained a different perspective as you witnessed part of the struggle a business owner experiences when people's lives and the company's survival is at stake. Laying people off is one of the most difficult struggles an owner could ever face. The negative impact layoffs have on employees and their families makes these types of decisions more devastating than can be expressed by mere words on a page. It was an attempt to give rare insight into how the process is carried out and the emotional toll it takes on both bosses and employees who lose their jobs.

**Other Approaches to Layoffs**

Not every boss is as caring and benevolent as the boss you just read about. Many bosses take widely differing approaches, including those who are: Frivolous, Favorite Players, All-Business, By-The-Book, Company-Men or Company-Women, and Bottom-Liners. Most, if not all of these approaches, are very common. However, there are additional approaches that border on the edge of insanity or criminality.

## Unscrupulous Approaches Some Bosses Take

These include the boss who is the...

1.    **Score-Settler**

"You hurt me, now it's my turn to hurt you."

2.    **Drill Sergeant**

"You are going to pay for all the stuff you have done."

3.    **Masochist**

"I love to see people suffer. It will be a pleasure to torture you and your family by laying you off."

4.    **Psycho**

"I am crazy. Nothing I do makes any sense. Neither will your layoff."

5.    **Incompetent**

"I am wishy-washy. Today you are fired, tomorrow you are hired."

6.    **Bigot**

"I don't like your type, your gender, your race, or your looks. I now have my chance to get rid of you, you are laid off."

7.    **Tyrant / Dictator**

"This is my company and I will run it any way I choose; there is absolutely nothing you or anyone else can do about it."

8.    **Other**

There are many additional types as well; fill in the blank...

## Defend Yourself?

The takeaway on this is that you can't successfully defend yourself against a weird boss. They will win every time. Any of them could complete their layoff list in two minutes or less. I think that some of them actually carry their completed lists around with them in their pockets while daring some unsuspecting employee to step out of line. The moment someone messes up, they are fired.

What do you do if you have a boss like one of those mentioned above?
1. Quietly do your job to the best of your ability
2. Make no waves and keep your nose clean
3. Maintain your sanity
4. Look for another job as soon as you are comfortable with that idea

## We Have Started Cracking The Layoff Code

This chapter may have cracked the layoff code for you. It may have simply started the cracking process for others. It did reveal a lot about how bosses think and make decisions about layoffs. Additional information will follow. As we end this chapter, my hope for you is that you have a benevolent boss. If you do, count yourself as being blessed. As you have seen, there are a gazillion people who work for bosses that are anything but benevolent.

You are in a position to gain several advantages over most of the other employees where you work. But remember, advantages are not accidental, they are planned. It will be up to you to seize every advantage you wish to use to begin layoff proofing yourself and your job.

In chapter four we will continue cracking the layoff code. Now, let's take a brief look at how layoffs are impacting you, your family, your friends, and all of America.

# Chapter 3
# A Snapshot of Layoffs in America

As far back as any person can remember there have been job layoffs. Throughout all of recorded business history, companies and businesses have experienced financial surges and retreats. Much like the ocean's tides, these surges and retreats are all simply functions of the economic climates dictated by the many factors which govern an economy. Consider the following examples. During the Great Depression of the 1920s and 1930s, the unemployment rate in America reached 25%. Contrast that with the figures of employment during World War II when employment rates of the available labor force averaged more than 90% and reached a high of 98.8%.

**Layoffs and Unemployment**

In America's recessionary economy, losing one's job will be a 100% unavoidable fact for millions of people. From November 2008, through April 2009, layoffs exceeded 544,000 people from America's 500 largest companies. This number doesn't include the hundreds of thousands of people laid off from thousands of smaller companies and businesses across America.

According to the Unites States Department of Labor, the recession began in December 2007. From the beginning of the recession, December 2007 through April 2009, there were 34,126 mass layoff events affecting some 3,498,427 people. A mass layoff occurs when 50 employees or more are laid off at the same time by the same employer. When all other layoffs are included, the numbers are much larger.

It is estimated that by May 2009, the total number of unemployed stood at 12.5 million people.

Unfortunately, 2009 and beyond will likely bring more of the same. In May and June, Chrysler and General Motors filed for bankruptcy and closed approximately three thousand auto dealerships. In addition, several of their assembly plants were closed. The net result left tens of thousands of people unemployed. The caveat is that no one knows just how severe this downturn may be, how long it will last, or when the economy can return to a semblance of normalcy. In addition, America's unemployment rate continues to increase. In June 2009, the US government placed the unemployment rate at 9.4 percent of the American workforce.

How long will unemployment continue to rise? While no one knows for certain what the future holds, it seems rather obvious that given the current economic situation and the long list of problems facing our economy for 2009 and beyond, the trend is for both layoffs and unemployment to continue to rise in the foreseeable future.

In reality, much could depend upon what course of action our financial institutions, Wall Street, and the United States government takes in response to our ever-worsening financial climate. The first quarter of 2009 saw a continuation of the downward slide in the overall economic picture.

## No-Fault Layoffs

When I was in middle school, my teacher had me go to the front of the class and write the following on the board 100 times: "I will not talk in class." You who have experienced a mass layoff should have to write: "It was NOT my fault." "It was NOT my fault." "It was NOT my fault." You should have to write it 100 times, or 500 times. You should have to write it until the truth finally sinks in that your layoff was not your fault. Mentally, you have already accepted that fact. Emotionally, you may still be struggling. Give your emotions some time, for it may take them a while to catch up with your thinking.

If you are someone who has been laid off, it is not necessarily your fault. In a later chapter we will discuss how some layoffs actually are the fault of the person being laid off. But for now, consider the fact that many small businesses and individually owned companies have had to lay people off in order to survive. It is one of the ugly facts of economic survival. If the company you work for can insure its survival by laying off 25% of its workforce, it has no choice but to do so. In fact, while it is extremely unpopular and causes a lot of pain, it does make good business sense to lay off 25% of its workforce in order to save the company as well as the jobs of the remaining 75% of its employees.

Thousands of small businesses and companies have been forced to lay off some of their employees. Thousands of others will be forced to do so. Some of those small businesses and companies will ultimately fail and be forced to go out of business. If you become one of the many unfortunate people who lose their jobs, you may be a victim of your company's scaling back its workforce to prevent its very demise.

Sadly, one of the facts of a lousy economy is that bad things happen. Unless you did something to contribute to your being laid off, you are not at fault. You are a victim of some extremely harsh financial circumstances. Does this make you feel any better? NO, not at all, being laid off feels terrible no matter what the cause. All the reasons in the world do not matter. It matters not that your company will ultimately survive the economic downturn. The fact remains…you don't have a job. Might you be hired back by your old company? Certainly, that is a possibility. The problem is this: no one knows when that may be. It could be anywhere from a few months to a few years. Again, there is no comfort in that scenario. In the last chapter we will further discuss ways to respond to layoff situations.

If you are the victim of a "no-fault" layoff, resist the temptation to waste your energies becoming angry with your former boss or company. Decide not to take it personally. Here's why: your boss was likely following orders laid down by his boss, who in turn may have been given those orders by an even higher boss. Get the picture. Your layoff had nothing to do with your value as a person, and it may have had nothing to do with your job performance either. Considering the poor climate of the U.S. economy, the layoff you have already experienced, or may yet experience, could have been a drastic step that was taken to insure the survival of your company.

This fact doesn't lessen your pain in any way. You and your family will definitely miss the money because your living expenses are ongoing and your monthly bills will continue to come in whether you are employed or not.

There are certain things employees do that set themselves up as likely candidates for layoffs. We will take a look at them next.

# Chapter 4
# Layoff Proof Your Job

As bosses begin the arduous task of deciding who they must lay off, they follow a process. This process follows sets of written and unwritten rules. Many larger companies have specific written policies and procedures governing layoffs that they follow to the letter. This affords legal protection should an employee accuse his former company of being unfair in the layoff process. But there is another side of the equation. Even though a large company may have a set of established guidelines for laying off part of the workforce, some follow subjective guidelines as well. These subjective guidelines are unwritten determinations that grant employers a great degree of latitude when it comes to choosing which employees will be laid off.

## Unwritten Lists for Job Layoffs

A great many bosses consult a specific list of people when it is time to begin layoffs. Your boss is very familiar with this list; in fact, he keeps his list with him 100% of the time. He never leaves home or work without it. He always takes his list when he is with his family at a restaurant, shopping, or at the movies. His list accompanies him when he is running, playing tennis, or golfing. He keeps his list with him when he goes on vacation, when he works in the yard, when he showers, and even when he sleeps. You ask: "Where does he keep his list, and why have I have never seen it?" You may be surprised to know that at this stage of the layoff process, his list is unwritten. It is a "mental list," that exists only in your boss's mind.

Believe me; you don't want your name on your boss's mental list. If a layoff is considered or needed, he begins creating his layoff list by drawing from the pool of employees' names he has in his mind. The names he selects are the names of the people he thinks the company could do without. At that point in the process the last name you want to have included on his mental layoff list is your name. When he begins putting names on paper, it is time to lay people off.

In the following pages you will find descriptions of workers common to most workplaces. You will recognize some of the people you work alongside every day. Depending upon how your company or boss sees things, your involvement in any one of them or any combination of them may cause you to be added to your boss's layoff list. At the same time, avoiding any one of them or any combination of them may prevent your name from even being considered for a layoff.

**Caution: Extremely Heavy Content Ahead**

Some extremely heavy and extremely personal content lies in the pages ahead. We started the layoff codecracking process by examining the boss's thinking, decision-making, and behavior. In the following pages you will find caricatures describing various types of problematic employees. The qualities that qualify them as problematic employees are their thinking, their decision-making, and their behavior. You will have no trouble envisioning many people you work alongside on a daily basis. A few may even cheer and take delight in the fact that some are getting what they deserve because someone is finally exposing them. Experience will confirm that these practices actually do result in layoffs and terminations.

As you examine the caricatures listed below, please consider the most difficult, emotional, and most personal part of the equation. Consider for a moment that the fait accompli or self-evident truth is the fact that your thinking, your decision-making, or your behavior could be causing problems with other people where you work, including your boss.

Some of the faces you see on the following pages may be the faces you are making as you look into the mirror and see yourself and your own behavior. However, any anger, frustration, discomfort, or emotional pain that you may experience will be worth it. Why, because if you really want to layoff proof yourself and your job, you will have to face the realities of what type of employee you are.

Should you be able to see yourself in any of the following descriptions, you will have placed yourself in a position to have further cracked the layoff code. Cracking this part of the code is designed to reveal personal practices you could be engaged in that could make you a likely target for a layoff or termination.

**Learn to Laugh at Yourself**

A few of the things you read may be upsetting because of their humor, sarcasm, or confrontational nature. Among the hardest things for me and you to see are our own faults, flaws, mistakes, and sins. These caricatures were not written in a spirit of condemnation. They were written as exposés of behaviors and practices that frequently result in people losing their jobs. Sometimes, the best way to deal with highly emotional and potentially negative subjects is to step back and laugh at oneself, other people, and the situation itself. Like me, every reader will be tempted to see everyone else but himself or herself in the following descriptions. Your natural reaction will be that of wanting to laugh at some of the people you work with when you see them described in the following pages. Laughing at someone else is fun...we do it all the time. But notice that I started with laughter first being directed at oneself. One of the greatest gifts anyone can have is that of not taking himself or herself too seriously. If you can laugh at yourself when you mess up or when someone tells a joke at your expense, people will have much more respect for you than if you get mad and sulk. Watching you getting mad or pouting will cause others to laugh more than ever. Relax, and laugh at yourself should others laugh at you. That will go far in improving your relationships with other people.

Have a little fun as you read the caricatures. They represent real people that I have either worked for, have worked alongside, or who have worked for me. Have some fun reading the list. Various people you know will come to mind. Share this list with some of your friends at work and enjoy a laugh or two. But be sure to have a good laugh or two at your own expense as well. As you read them you will likely see yourself in more of these caricatures than you may want to admit.

## Boss' Master List of People Targeted for Layoffs

1.   **The Newbie**: "The last to be hired is the first to be fired."
2.   **The Slacker**: "Workers who are nonproductive are out the door."
3.   **The Baby**: "Everyone is really getting tired of babysitting him."
4.   **Mr. Incompetent**: "He either can't or is not doing his job."
5.   **The Whiner**: "She's a whiner on a mission…a perpetual pity party."
6.   **The Manipulator**: "He does nothing but manipulate our other employees."
7.   **The Gripe Machine**: "All she ever does is constantly complain about everything. I have nicknamed her 'The Gripe Machine.'"
8.   **The Spoon**: "He can't get along with other employees: all he ever does is stir things up or keep them stirred up."
9.   **Mr. Negative**: "He has nothing to offer but a negative attitude."
10.  **Ms. Undependable**: "She is just not a dependable employee."

11. **Sneaky Snake**: "He is so untrustworthy and sneaky."
12. **Sticky Fingers**: "He's always stealing from the company: money, time, or materials."
13. **The Liar**: "The only thing I can say about her is that she's a liar."
14. **The Sexual Harasser**: "Has the guy never heard of sexual harassment charges?"
15. **Potty Mouth**: "His words are an indicator of his substandard vocabulary."
16. **Ms. Unreliable**: "She really doesn't want to work: she is always late, leaving early, or asking off."
17. **The Surfer**: "We are paying him to work, not surf the Internet."
18. **Mr. Break Room Manager**: "He always hangs out in the break room. 'Where's Bill, let me guess...?'"
19. **Ms. Socialite: the MIA**: "She can never be found when you need her."
20. **Lazy Susan**: "She never pulls her weight around the workplace."
21. **The Mirage**: "He only works when he sees me coming."
22. **Ms. Two-Faced**: "She says one thing to my face and another behind my back."
23. **The Tattler**: "You should have heard her the other day. 'Hey boss, do you know what Stacey just...'"
24. **The Judge**: "She thinks she works here to judge everyone."
25. **The Jury**: "Don't confuse him with the facts; his mind is already made up about everything."
26. **The Executioner**: "The guy is ruthless in the way he treats other people."
27. **Mr. Universe**: "He is the most inconsiderate person I have ever had work for me."
28. **Mr. Superiority**: "He never helps out with other people's projects: he thinks he's just too good for everyone else."

29. **The Text Berry**: "All I ever get is a busy signal. She takes her phone off the hook and spends most of her time on her Text Berry."
30. **Ms. Gossip**: "She's the owner of the gossip and rumor mills around here."
31. **The Favor Granter:** "All I ever hear about her is that she provides 'favors' to some of the guys from the office."
32. **Mr. Contraband**: "The guy is always on the borderline of being illegal."
33. **Mr. Put-Down**: "You wouldn't believe what that guy said to me a couple of years ago."

You just read the short list of 33 behaviors and practices that could cause you to lose your job. They will be discussed in greater detail in the following pages.

When a subjective boss begins writing down the names of the people he wants to lay off, if you happen to fit any one or any combination of these descriptions, you may be added to his layoff list. At the same time, NOT DOING some of them or any combination of them may prevent your name from even being considered as an addition to his list.

### Do You Want to Layoff Proof Yourself and Your Job?

If you answered yes, I have one more question. How badly do you want to reach that goal? If you are waiting for someone else, or for a certain set of circumstances to come along and make you layoff proof, you are wasting your time. The only way you will ever enjoy a high degree of job security is for you to take charge of your life, your job, and your personal work-ethic. One of the principles of success in the workplace is that you are in charge of your performance as an employee. Now is the time for you to step up to the plate and take charge of yourself, your job, your performance, your attitude, your behavior, your work-ethic, and your career. Only you can layoff proof yourself and your job. Are you ready to step up and begin the process that could have a positive impact upon the rest of your career?

## There are No Guarantees but Your Chances are Good

Understand that there is no guarantee that if you eliminate these issues you will keep your job. While there are no guarantees, your chances are good. If you will follow the proven results-oriented principles that have worked for millions of people through the ages, you can layoff proof yourself. We will consider them in greater detail in a moment.

Common sense dictates that there are many things you can do to insure that you will NOT be among the first persons who come to mind when your boss gets ready to start laying off or firing employees.

With hard work and creativity you can insure that your name is placed on your boss's "preferred" list. This is your boss's "good" mental list. It is the list of people he or she wishes to keep as employees no matter what the cost.

## A Closer Look at These 33 Unwritten Descriptions

Again, here is the boss' layoff list. Take a closer look at the categories that can spawn layoffs for certain employees. The boss portrayed in our scenario is a boss who is an equal opportunity "un-employer." He is not afraid to lay anyone off for any of the following reasons.

## Accidental Layoff

## 1.    The Newbie

Seniority: "The last to be hired is the first to be fired." You need to know that your layoff is not your fault. Your layoff is nothing but an economic and timing issue. It simply stands to reason that if you are the person who is the most recent to be hired by a business or a company, you will be among the most likely candidates to be the first to go if your company decides to implement a layoff strategy. My son became a victim of seniority when he and dozens of other new employees were furloughed from their nationwide company in February 2009. Your layoff is not your fault, since you were the last person hired you will now be the first person laid off. If you need to assign blame, blame the poor economy or recession.

## Layoffs Waiting to Happen

### 2. The Slacker

"The guy should buy a new pair of slacks and wear them to work in order to commemorate the fact that he is a 'slacker.'" From the business owner's perspective, this is a guaranteed layoff. Workers who are nonproductive are among the first out the door. If you are a person who is not pulling your share of the weight on your job, you will be among the first to come to mind when it is time to start laying people off. Many workers who are unproductive are among the first to be shown the door. A lot of employees just don't get it. They have never understood the simple dictum that they are there to work. Work can be many different things to different people. For some, work is little more than a ticket to a paycheck. For others, work is one of those necessary evils that they despise but feel that they have to do to in order to keep their bills paid. To a select group, work is nothing more than a place to socialize. To many, work is seen as a place to produce a product, to offer a service, to sell goods or services, or to make a contribution to something larger than them. Many successful people consider their work as a gift they have been given to meet a variety of other peoples' needs. For a select few, their job is an opportunity to improve or sharpen their skills while helping their company or business.

In short, if you are not making a contribution to your company or business in some significant way, you may be in line for a layoff or termination. To better understand your boss's situation, ask yourself the following question and give a 100% honest answer: If you owned your own company and made all your own hiring decisions, would you hire someone exactly like yourself to come and work for you? If you were forced to answer "no," then you are a person who could use some improvement in the area of productivity. Stop right now and write down 10 things you can begin doing at work which will improve your productivity. Believe me; your boss will notice.

## 3.    The Baby

Babies are wonderful, but not if the baby is an employee at work. Everyone, bosses and fellow employees alike, grow tired of babysitting an employee. I have never met a boss who enjoys being a babysitter when the object of his babysitting was an employee. If you are someone who always has to be told what to do next, you may be a good candidate for a layoff. Why should someone else have to spend a portion of their valuable time telling you what to do next? Have you not considered coming up with some things to do at work on your own? "Now how old did you say you were? Do you carry a pacifier around with you everywhere you go?"

Consider the term "self-starter." Managers usually love an employee that can take a job, determine what needs to be done, set appropriate goals, establish priorities, and then produce results by accomplishing what they set out to do. These employees are valued by their managers and bosses, for they never have to spend time worrying whether they are doing their job effectively.

Unless you are new at your job and still learning what you are supposed to do, the people you work with shouldn't have to coach you. If you have been with the company for any length of time you should be able to recognize what needs to be done and then do it. Make a turnaround starting today. Stop being someone who has to be babysat. Turn up your performance level. Increase your production. Take charge of your job and give it your very best effort. Complete your job responsibilities first, and then begin looking for things you can do. Set a goal and make a game of amazing your boss with your new resolve and productivity. See how quickly he notices the new you.

The flip-side: some employees have the misfortune of working for a micro-manager. Micros come with varying degrees of control obsessions. A major control freak can make your life miserable. In essence, they are the baby sitter and you are the baby. You are the baby to be babysat no matter how productive or efficient you are. Your abilities may exceed those of your boss, but you are being micro-managed into oblivion. It is something you resent and see as a putdown. Don't take it personally, you may just be in the wrong place at the wrong time and you may have to stay there and make the most of a bad situation. If you deal with a micro-manager on a consistent basis you may wish to consider other options...starting with changing jobs.

### 4.   Mr. Incompetent

"He either can't or is not doing his job." Are you in control of your job or does your job control you? Your inability to do your job may be a result of being undisciplined and loving it, lacking the proper training or skills to do the job, or a sense of disgust with your job in general. You may need to spend your next day off from work mapping a strategy by which you can gain control of your job. Being in control of your job means:

1.   You have a good understanding of your primary task.
2.   You clearly define and understand what is expected of you.
3.   You set limits as to what you will and will not do as part of your job.
4.   You set goals which you expect to meet.
5.   You develop a personal strategy to help you achieve the goals and results you want to accomplish.

6.    You develop a personal action plan which will enable you to put your strategy into action.

Many "incompetent" people are not really incompetent at all. The main problem they struggle with is that they are not in control of their job; their job is in control of them. Step up and control something...control your job performance. Ramp up your output or productivity; it will be noticed.

There is one thing you can do which will have an immediate impact upon you and the people around you. Organize and clean up your workspace. An unorganized workspace shouts that you lack self-discipline. A friend of mine came into the office one day to see a placard someone had placed on his cluttered desk: "He who has a dirty desk wears dirty underwear." The next day, his desk was spotless. A disorganized or cluttered workspace says that you are far from being in control. "But, organizing is not one of my gifts." So what? You were not born knowing how to ride a bicycle, ski, drive, or operate a computer. All of those are learned skills. Clean up your workspace tomorrow and get organized. Stop copping out. I guarantee that the boss will notice, and it will leave him or her with the impression that you are in control. Your space may not look like the Taj Mahal, but chances are that you can make it look better than it does now.

Two final suggestions: write out a to-do list every afternoon before you leave for home, or first thing every morning before you begin work, and create a system by which you can prioritize your work. This will allow you to do the most important jobs first while relegating the less important jobs to later in the day or the next day.

## 5.    The Whiner

"She's a whiner on a mission...a perpetual pity party. She sounds like my whining cat when she whines about her schedule or workload." Have you ever heard someone jokingly ask another person: "Would you like a little cheese with that whine?" Grow up. The only people who might like whiners are other whiners, and the only reason they might like other whiners is that not many other people would like them except other whiners. I'm not sure that whiners like one another; they may just need someone to listen to their whining. Adults expect babies to whine because whining is normal for a baby. When you reach adulthood, some of your childish behaviors need to be left behind. The Bible says: "When I was a child, I talked like a child, I thought like a child, I reasoned like a child. When I became a man, I put childish ways behind me" I Corinthians 13:11 (NIV).

Many people get wrapped up in their own personal pity parties. Involving yourself in these will do nothing to further your cause at work. Surprise everyone you work with and stop whining. It may be a very difficult habit to break, but you can do it. Make a list of a few things that you whine about. Next, develop a strategy of what you will do the next time that particular situation presents itself. Try something like replacing your whining with a compliment to someone. If you just can't bring yourself to give someone a compliment, try doing something else which you would like to substitute. Do you whine to your supervisor or boss? Chances are that they are sick of your whining. Show them that you can stop this destructive behavior.

Finally, try going for a full 30 minutes without whining about something. Next, stretch it to one hour, then two, then four. Finally, you will be able to make it for a full day. People will notice. Keep it up.

## 6.   The Manipulator

"He does nothing but tries and manipulates our other employees. The guy needs a scrambled Rubik's cube on his desk to manipulate when he feels like manipulating someone." People grow sick and tired of being manipulated. This person seemingly has a mental disorder. They are always attempting to turn circumstances, events, and people toward themselves. They are champions when it comes to being self-centered. Their lofty expectations are designed to expect that everything should revolve around them.

Getting someone to do their work for them and using people are two of their hallmarks. It is obvious that they don't care about anyone but themselves because they see others as merely stepping stones to help them get ahead of everyone else.

Manipulators are not to be trusted. Normally, they are negative people and their motives are easily seen through. They are not to be befriended. You are better off having as little to do with them as possible. One of their main goals is to "play" everyone who will allow them to do so.

It is funny because they think that they fly under everyone else's radar. How sadly mistaken they are. Most people can spot them a mile away. Do yourself a major favor and steer clear of them. Chances are that the boss is on to their little game and you don't want to run the risk of guilt by association. Neither do you want to be seen as a collaborator. Manipulate the manipulator by staying away from them. When layoffs come to your workplace you don't want to be anywhere near this person or they will either take you down with them or will set you up as the person who takes the fall. They will figure out a way to manipulate things so that you will get the pink slip and they stay on to continue doing their dirty work.

If you are a manipulator and want to change, begin by asking yourself why you always want to manipulate people. Once you figure out the answer, you can take definite steps to change your behavior. A few things you can begin doing now which will bring change: start doing your own work instead of trying to get another to do it for you. Offer to help others with their work. After they get over the initial shock they may allow you to help. Begin seeing yourself as a team member, not a one man or one woman star of the show.

## Bad Attitudes Rise to the Top

### 7. The Gripe Machine

"All she ever does is constantly complain about everything. I am about ready to hang a sign on her cubicle that says 'Complaint Department,' it has gotten so bad that I have nicknamed her 'The Gripe Machine.'" This person is so much like the whiner, they could be their twin. Some people complain about everything. That is the chronic complainer in action. Everyone is sick and tired of your constant griping and chronic complaining. If you are a complainer and find it hard to get along with your boss you may save your job by learning a new behavior. Learn how to check your negative feelings and complaints at the door when you clock in. If you are a complainer at work, chances are that you are a complainer at home as well. Learn to leave your negativity and complaining in the car on the way to and from work. If you have worked at your job for any significant amount of time, unless your boss is a total numbskull, he knows what kind of attitude you have.

If you are constantly complaining to your boss and other superiors, you are in line for a layoff or termination. Why? Getting rid of your negative comments and negative attitude is a positive change that they, along with most of your co-workers would welcome.

Ask yourself the following question. Has my complaining accomplished anything positive for me or my boss? Write down your five biggest gripes or complaints. Next, write down some things that you can do to solve them. Accept responsibility for your own actions. Refuse to palm them off onto someone else. If you can't get along with your boss, stop complaining and develop strategies to get along with him or her.

### 8. The Spoon

"About the only thing he ever does is to stir things up or keep them stirred up. He is nothing but a troublemaker.

I have nicknamed him 'The spoon.'" Do you enjoy stirring things up or keep them stirred up at work? If your company implements layoffs you may need to begin looking for your free ticket out the door. "But I cooperate with other people." Forget it. The only people you cooperate with are other troublemakers. You have built quite a reputation for yourself. Since the boss calls you the "spoon," what kind of spoon are you, a measuring spoon, a cooking spoon, or a plastic spoon? The only reason I ask is because this may give you a clue as to how much you will be missed when you are laid off.

Are you known at work as a uniter or a divider? Are you someone who stirs up trouble at work? Do you enjoy seeing people get fired up for all the wrong reasons? Are you the type of employee that people dread seeing coming, or are you someone that people like to see and enjoy talking with? If you are known around the office or plant as someone that can't get along with the other employees what makes you think that your boss would really want to keep you around the workplace any longer than he would have to? You may respond by saying that your knowledge or contribution you make to your company is too valuable for them to lay you off or terminate you. You may be right. You may be tolerated because of what you contribute to the company. Don't ever let this be said of you: "He or she can't get along with other people."

Write down five things that you can personally implement to enable yourself to get along better with the other employees. Ask yourself the following question. "How may I redirect my energies and attitudes to accomplish positive results for the company and my fellow employees?" The biggest changes needed are probably within you. Focus upon what you can change. Refuse to focus on the changes others need to make. If you keep stirring things up you may get your free ticket out the door.

## 9.   Mr. Negative

"He has nothing to offer but a negative attitude. This guy would find something negative to say if you gave him a million dollars." Don't you just love negative people? "Is that supposed to be some kind of a joke," you ask? Yes, a sarcastic joke. Negative people are everywhere. Chances are you know several of them at the place where you work. Hopefully, the most negative person you deal with on a daily basis is not your boss. Along with many of you, I once worked for a boss like that myself. Negative people are in a habit of interjecting a dark cloud into almost every situation they touch or comment upon. They are no fun to be around. Nothing is ever right; nothing ever suits them or meets their standards. They always have some snide remark about everyone and every situation.

Only a negative person could receive a dozen roses and find something wrong with them. They could receive a certificate for a free meal for two at their favorite restaurant only to find something wrong with the meal. Some readers would rather have a root canal than have to deal with a negative coworker, boss, or supervisor any longer.

Are you the negative person I am talking about? Do you see the worst of every situation? Do you frequently criticize the other people you work with? Do you never give a compliment to anyone? Do you always find fault with what others are doing? If so, then you are a part of the problem. People are sick of your negative attitude and your negative criticisms. I have a suspicion that you may also be sick of your negativity as well. It is time for change. Give it up and stop being so negative. You may know that you are mostly negative and take great delight in it, or you may be oblivious to your own actions. One problem many negative people have is that they don't think that they are negative.

Here is a very simple two-part strategy which can enable you to stop being so negative. You can implement this strategy beginning today. Begin by learning to keep your negative statements to yourself. Another, but not so tactful way of saying this is: learn to keep your mouth shut. Here is where you can poke some fun at yourself. When a situation arises where you would normally say something negative, don't utter a single word. Watch your co-workers' faces. They may cringe while they wait for you to say something negative. They will surely wonder why you didn't give your usual two-cents-worth. Keep your mouth shut. Once you see their surprised looks, you can burst out laughing at yourself and tell them that you know what a sap you have been. The first time you do this they may not laugh along with you, but by the second or third time you tell them you have been a sap and keep laughing at yourself, they will join in. This will bring you some much-needed acceptance as they see you "eating crow."

Want to have some more fun? If you would like to see the shock on some people's faces implement the second part of the dual strategy. Give someone an honest compliment. They will be shocked and their mouth may fly open. When it does, say something like: "I'm sorry I have been so negative, but I am trying to change. I really meant it when I said that you did do a good job when you _____." You can have some fun with this one for they surely will never expect it. Compliment someone's good work, their neat office, or the way they handled a certain situation. Learn to find legitimate reasons to compliment someone. Turn this into a constructive game for yourself. Your "road to recovery," can blend some fun with cognitive behavior reorientation.

You can change. It will take some time, but you can do it. You have a good motivation, because highly negative or critical people find themselves rising to the top of many people's layoff lists.

## Character Issues Can Make or Break you

### 10.   Ms. Undependable

"Have you noticed that Kim seems to be always call-ing in sick, and that Kayla is always leaving early?" "Yes, I have noticed. We really do need to address those situations before they get any worse. What's up with Jennifer always asking to be off lately?" You just overheard a conversation between two supervisors as they were checking their de-partment work schedules for the next two weeks. They no-tice your work habits. Without exception, each boss keeps a mental, and sometimes written, list of such things.

When it comes to dependability, you are on your boss's list. The question is: which list are you on? Are you on the list of people who are dependable and never miss work unless they are really sick? Or, are you on your boss's list of people whom he has labeled as undependable? Every boss has his own personal list. If you don't believe me...no, on second thought, don't dare ask. Your boss may tell you that you are on his list.

I have heard people say something like: "Mary must be very sick today because she never misses work." I have also heard people say something like: "Oh, Bill is not here again, that doesn't surprise me any because he is always missing work."

How dependable are you at your job? Are you con-stantly calling in sick? One way to answer that question ob-jectively is to look at how many sick leave days you took last year. Did you use all your sick leave, half of it, or none of it? There will always be some unusual exceptions, but almost every person will have a few days per year when either they or someone in their family is sick and they can't go to work. Parents who have young children must have someone stay with them when they are sick and have to miss school. Oth-ers have elderly parents or spouses who require extra care or medical attention and most bosses understand these realities so long as they are not abused. The best way to approach your superiors is to be honest with them and provide documentation for the times when you must miss work.

Another gauge of your dependability is whether you are constantly leaving work early or asking for extra time off. Most bosses are keenly aware of these practices and make mental lists of people who abuse the privileges offered by your company or business.

How brave are you? Ask a trusted friend to be totally honest with you and tell you what other people say about you when you are away from work because of sickness. Ask them to tell you what others say behind your back when it comes to your asking to leave work early or take extra time off. You may be surprised by what you hear. But be careful and don't lose a friend or damage a friendship over this. You may not think it is worth that extreme.

The point here is not to embarrass you or to hurt your feelings. The point is to enable you to get a better picture of how you are perceived by your boss and make any necessary improvements that may be needed.

Being undependable will rocket you to the top of your boss's list of potential layoffs. When it comes time to pare back the workforce, you will be in the top 10 people who come to mind. The key to overcoming this predicament is to change your boss's perception of you from being among his undependable people to that of being among his most dependable. Only you can make this change in perception possible. Remember, perception is reality to most people. What they perceive is what they will believe.

## 11. Sneaky Snake

"The guy is so sneaky that the other day I thought about putting a pair of my old sneakers on his desk." See how you rate in this department. Ron, your boss, just bought a new Corvette and needs someone to drive it to the dealership for its 5,000 mile checkup. Are you the type of person your boss could trust with his keys to have the work done? How trustworthy are you? What if your boss was getting ready to enter a meeting with her regional manager only to suddenly realize that she left a key confidential file lying on the kitchen table at her house? Since she has to have the file and must start the meeting in five minutes, could she trust you to drive to her house, pick up the file, and bring it back to her without looking at its contents?

Are you untrustworthy? Are you sneaky and do you snoop around at work? Are the other employees suspicious of you and of your actions? Do you make it your business to look at other employees' personal information when they step away from their computers or workspace? When a coworker misses work, do you rummage through his or her desk and filing cabinets to see what you can find? If you think that no one knows that you do these things you are kidding yourself. People notice what is taking place at work. They pay attention to what you and others do with their work and free times.

If you are brave, ask a trusted friend to be honest with you and tell you what others think of your trustworthiness. Trust that is lost or damaged must be re-earned. You will have to reestablish the fact that you can be trusted. Reputations can be rebuilt. Here's how you may start rebuilding yours. First, write out a list of five things that will enable you to regain the trust of your supervisor, boss, and fellow employees. Next, put those five action items in effect starting today. Third, concentrate upon rebuilding a sense of trustworthiness. You will be glad you did.

## 12.  Sticky Fingers

"I honestly believe the guy's motto is: 'Everybody steals from the company so why shouldn't I get my part?' He must dip his fingers in glue every morning before he comes to work." Is this employee correct in his assumption that everyone steals from the company? As someone who has worked in retail, I can assure you that not everyone steals from their company.

Beth was secure in her job as a cashier in a major retail company. She was efficient, accurate, and so trusted that she was placed in an area where cash refunds were made to customers. She worked there for many months before money started missing. Beth just knew that she had come up with the perfect way to steal money. She chose to rationalize her stealing as giving herself a well-deserved raise. Her scheme was simple; she would return customers' merchandise whose receipts showed that they had paid with cash. Instead of giving their receipts back, Beth would retain them and, when no one was looking, return the merchandise again and pocket the cash. It only took her supervisor two days to catch on to her little trick. She allowed her to continue stealing for a few more days and captured all the transactions on video. One day she was summoned to the manager's office, confronted by regional loss prevention personnel, ushered out of the store, and prosecuted. She paid back all the money to avoid jail time, but was terminated for stealing.

Have employees stolen from any of the companies where I have worked? Yes. What happened to them? Some were prosecuted, but all were terminated. Theft is not only common in retail, it is more common in large corporations than many care to admit. Stealing takes place at all levels. People steal from the top down: from corporate CEOs and executives, to business owners and managers, all the way down to hourly employees. For many, stealing is a way of life. Not all stealing focuses upon money. While many steal merchandise or money, others steal time, products, materials, Social Security numbers, and peoples' identities. Some steal ideas or proprietary information and a few steal securities.

Other forms of stealing involve stealing customers or accounts. In various arenas where sales generate commissions, some workers have developed ways of stealing other employees' sales and commissions. Some steal the credit for an innovative idea or an invention. These practices have resulted in the firings of many employees. Companies just don't take well to stealing, regardless of its form. How would you rate yourself when it comes to stealing? Ask yourself the following question. "If every employee stole the same amount that I steal what impact would it have upon the company?"

The final way of stealing to be mentioned is one of the most serious of all, stealing another person's reputation. You can offer to pay for any merchandise or commissions you may have stolen. You can offer to repay any cash or materials you may have taken in order to avoid prosecution. However, it is almost impossible for a person to rebuild his or her reputation to the level it once enjoyed after it has been damaged. For example, suppose that you work as a cashier at Starbucks and $20 comes up missing at the end of your shift. You take pride in your honesty and know that you did not take the money. However, the real culprit, the one who actually stole the money blames you in order to cover his tracks. Not only does he blame you, he does it in a loud, public, and embarrassing manner so that everyone in the store may hear. Two days later the manager quietly approaches you and says that he knows you didn't steal the money. He says they know who stole it but they are going to give him a second chance and allow him to continue working for the company. Guess what? In some people's minds, you are still guilty. As long as you work there, some will consider you a thief. Your reputation has been stolen. No matter what you say or do, you will be unable to convince some of the other employees that you didn't take the money. It is not fair in any way. But it is reality.

Never get caught up in the game of stealing another person's property or reputation. Don't steal from your company or business. This game is deadly and may result in termination and or prosecution. How does one stop stealing? Before you can stop stealing you must want to stop. Old habits are hard to break. There are several solutions including the following two that I have listed. The first is to stop stealing by going cold-turkey. This means that you tell yourself to stop stealing and you just stop stealing. That method will work for many people. If it doesn't work for you, consider the next option. Ask a trusted friend to become an accountability partner. Have them ask you this same question every day: "Tom, did you steal anything today?" For this to work you must give an honest answer. The honest answer leads us to the next reason people experience layoffs.

## 13.  The Liar

"You never know when _____ is telling the truth. About the only thing I can say about her is that she is a liar. 'Liar, liar, pants on fire.'" One of the bedrock principles of business is that of being able to rely upon someone to tell the truth. If being honest and telling the truth is a problem for you, it is something you need to address immediately. Ask a co-worker to rate you on truth-telling if you have any doubts about how you rank in this area.

Everyone has a reputation. Your reputation is basically the sum total of who you are as seen by other people. A good reputation is to be highly valued as one of your greatest assets. A poor or damaged reputation is something to be avoided. A poor or damaged reputation can be repaired or rebuilt, but rebuilding your reputation will take some time. It is much easier to lose someone's trust than it is to gain it back.

Bosses view liars as basically dishonest people. They have it figured this way: "If he will lie to me about a small thing, he will lie to me about anything." There is a quick-fix for this problem. Always tell the truth. In the courtroom a witness takes an oath whereby they swear to "tell the truth, the whole truth, and nothing but the truth." Be honest at work. Be honest at home. Be honest with God. Be honest with everyone. Even if it costs you, be honest.

If you feel that your boss and co-workers see you as a liar and you wish to change their perception, there is something you can do beginning now. Start telling the truth, the whole truth, and nothing but the truth. It will take some time, but you can earn their trust and begin to witness a change in their thinking.

How does one stop lying? As in stealing, old habits are hard to break. Before you can stop lying you must want to stop. There are several solutions including the following two. The first is to stop lying by going cold-turkey. This means that you tell yourself to stop lying and you just stop lying. That method will work for many people. If it doesn't work for you, consider asking a trusted friend to become your accountability partner. Have them ask you this same question every day: "Cassie, did you lie about anything today?" For this method to be successful, you must be willing to give a completely honest answer each and every time your accountability partner asks.

## 14.  The Sexual Harasser

"He always is putting his hands where he shouldn't. Has the guy never heard of sexual harassment charges?" This practice will not only get you fired, you can be sued. Not all workplace sexual harassment will lead to litigation. However, that doesn't mitigate the fact that it is a serious offense that can have very serious consequences.

I am not implying that a sexual harasser at work will end up like this, but I recently received a Sex Offender Notification mail-out from my local Sheriff's Department. The announcement included the name, photograph, address, criminal charges, and other pertinent personal information announcing the fact that a sexual deviant just moved into my zip code. Think about how humiliating it would be should one of your coworkers receive a document highlighting your photograph and criminal charges in the mail. Have you never heard of sexual harassment charges? Many have gone down this road from riches to rags. These charges can be career-ending. One is well served by keeping his hands and his words to himself or herself.

Tim was better looking than average and thought he was a gift to women. His remarks were often sexual in nature. He often spoke in the code of the double entendre, using words and sentences which could be taken in more than one way. Women were very uncomfortable around Tim. He was the center of discussion on more than one occasion. His break came when a brave employee reported that he had fondled her. At first, her claim was summarily dismissed and treated very casually. As word began to leak throughout the company, other women came forward and said that they had also been fondled by Tim. Tim lost his job, was prosecuted, and is having a difficult time finding employment.

A word of warning: sexual harassment is not limited just to touching another person. It can and does include suggestive words or phrases, displaying certain paraphernalia or printed materials, suggestive language or behavior, sexual jokes or humor, and a variety of other things. You will best serve yourself by refusing to engage in any questionable activity which might be construed as having anything to do with sexual harassment. One of the fastest ways to be terminated is to be involved in this type of behavior. Bosses aren't very keen about having sexual harassers on the payroll.

Sexual harassment issues may require professional counseling. If you are a victim, or have engaged in this behavior, you may wish to seek counsel immediately.

### 15.  Potty Mouth

In many settings, violation of this principle may not cost you your job. However, your vocabulary says a lot about you. "He sure has a foul mouth," or "Can you believe that she has such a 'potty mouth.'" What a compliment? Four letter words are disgusting. Someone rightly said that profanity is an indicator of a less-than-average vocabulary. I repeat, your vocabulary says a lot about you. Profanity may come from a sense of frustration, anger, habit, or just wanting to fit in. Regardless of its source, it is a deeply engrained habit for far too many people. It says a lot more about you than you may realize. "What about freedom of speech," you say? You are right; you have the freedom to refuse to use profanity. We are blessed to live in a country where people can say almost anything they wish without fear of retribution. However, there are a few exceptions. You can be jailed for threatening the life of the President, as well as a few other free speech issues. Even high school, college, and professional athletes and coaches have to watch what they say or they will be ejected from the game. Speech is free, but it does matter what you say.

Profanity is so widespread that it has almost become a second language. It is virtually impossible to find a show on TV which doesn't contain four letter words in the script. Many movies leave you feeling like you have just taken a tour through your city's sewer. Music videos and many songs are filled with four letter words. Profanity is so common that it has permeated most work places. One never used to hear women and children using profanity, but now even that is commonplace.

Daycare workers are the first to hear it...right out of the mouths of toddlers. What do you expect? Children hear their parents using it and they hear it on virtually every prime time TV program and many cartoons. Kids grow up using profanity, thinking it makes them seem tough or more grown up. Many carry this over into the teen years and then into their careers. The best way to teach your kids to use profanity is for them to hear you using it in front of them.

Profanity is totally unacceptable behavior in many work settings. Use of four letter words will definitely keep you from receiving promotions and certain job assignments in some companies. While profanity may be acceptable and widely used in other companies, its use does make you sound like a person with less than average intelligence. Computer programmers use an acrostic: GIGO. Garbage In Garbage Out. Limit what you allow in and it will be easier to control what comes out of your mouth.

How does one clean up his language? One of the simplest and best ways would be to make its use cost you something valuable. What would you do if you had to pay a co-worker $5 every time you used a four letter word? A few $50 days would get your attention wouldn't they? "Heck yes," you say. See, you have already cleaned up your language.

### 16.  Ms. Unreliable

A person who is routinely late for work, leaves early, or is asking off work may as well paint a target on their back. "I don't think she really wants to work, she's always late, leaving early, or asking for more time off. She does this at least one or two days per week. She would win the excuse-making contest if we were to have one." Being fashionably late only works in the movies. There is nothing fashionable about being late for work, nor is there anything glorious about leaving early or asking to be off more than your allotted vacation time permits.

The average person will be late for work occasionally. Most of the times a person is late can be attributed to things which are beyond their control. It might be heavy traffic, a car crash, a stalled car, a flat tire, or a transit strike. Those are unforeseen circumstances which are unavoidable.

While being on time 100% of the time is almost impossible, some have managed to accomplish that. The circumstances which are avoidable: oversleeping, bad weather or stopping on the way to work to buy gas are the ones which can cause you a problem with your boss. Why should he care? Because he knows that with a little extra effort, you could have planned ahead and been on time.

I once worked for an airline that had a zero tolerance policy for being late. Everyone who worked there knew the policy and it was extremely rare that someone was late. In the rare instance that someone was late they were credited with having an "occurrence." If they collected three in a given 12 month period, they were terminated from their job. I saw only one person terminated for being late to work the entire time I worked for the airline. To insure that we would be on time for work, everyone followed a relatively simple plan; we all arrived early and clocked in ahead of time.

A friend who works at a nationally branded retail store told me about a young father who was recently terminated for constantly calling in sick and being late for work. It seems that the man had either been "sick" or late for work as many as a dozen times. The manager finally terminated him. It does happen.

You can teach yourself to be on time for work. It may take some drastic measures such as going to bed earlier or, if you are in a habit of tapping the snooze button on your clock and falling back to sleep, try using a second alarm clock. With some extra self-discipline you can do it.

## 17.  The Surfer

"He's always on the Internet. We are paying him to work, not to surf. The other day when I told him to 'hang ten,' he shot me a dirty look."

Scores of people are terminated for Internet abuse in American companies every week. You are being paid to work, not to be a cyber surfer. I have heard of more than one incident where an individual was fired for running his own Internet business from his computer terminal while working his day job. Once discovered, they were all terminated. Oh, you should have seen the shock and disbelief on their faces when they were told that they had been discovered.

Most companies have the capability to know what you do and which sites you visit when you are on the Internet. Surprised? You shouldn't be. You are being paid to work for the company that employed you, not to check your email, visit your favorite websites, or run your own Internet business.

Recently, my wife and I were in one of the ubiquitous gift shops in Gatlinburg. We couldn't help but notice that the clerk was preoccupied with his laptop. I looked to see what was captivating his attention and found that it was an Internet gaming site he was visiting. Totally immersed in an online game, he also totally ignored the customers who were in the store. Obviously, he was an hourly employee, for had he been the owner he would have been engaging his customers and attempting to sell them some merchandise. As I watched him play and kill the monsters that were trying to zap him, I couldn't help but wonder how many people walked out the door with free merchandise under their arms because this poor chap was so mesmerized that he never would have noticed. Some of you have probably seen the same guy and had the very same thoughts I had.

Chances are that your boss has a pretty good idea how you spend your computer time. Most large companies have IT departments that monitor web time and email content. Even if your company doesn't monitor your computer time, other employees know how you spend time on your computer, and you know that people do like to talk.

What you do on your computer at home is your own business. But you need to know that thousands of people have been terminated for visiting porn sites or for sending either offensive or personal emails. You should have a clear understanding of your company's computer and Internet use policies and abide by them.

How do you overcome this liability? Again, stop cold-turkey, get an accountability partner, or have IT remove Internet access from your terminal.

## 18. Mr. Break Room Manager

You are having a rough day at work and you look forward to just a few minutes away from the phone, customers, assembly line, or other responsibilities. Your break time finally arrives and you make your way to your company's break room for a soda or cup of coffee and a snack. A strange thing happens when you enter the door. You hear your name being used in a sentence followed by the words: "...break room manager." Who is the break room manager at your company? That is a standard joke at countless companies around America. I hope that this joke is not told at your expense.

What exactly is a "break room manager," anyway? It is a pejorative used to describe a person who can always be found on break in the company break room. The idea is that you are in the break room so often that you have been assigned the duty to monitor the activities and comings and goings of the company break room. This title is not one to be sought after, so how can you avoid gaining this reputation? The answer is simple. Take only the number of breaks that are allowed, and never abuse the allotted time. Employees who are constantly abusing privileges are usually noticed and labeled as privilege abusers. Their names float to the top of the layoff list. If your reputation is firmly cemented and you wish to repair it, what can you do? To repair a damaged reputation, stay away from the break room and take short breaks at your desk for several weeks. When you resume your break room visits three months later, you will have changed your reputation for the better.

Another gem of wisdom concerning the company break room. Be judicious concerning your conversations when on break. People will often repeat what they hear in such public settings. If someone hears you running another employee down, that person will form an opinion of you and it probably will not be a good one. If you have problems with your boss or supervisor, you may wish to keep those problems to yourself. If you tell your woes to someone willing to commiserate with you, your conversation may have repercussions. Suppose you are critical of your supervisor or boss, and later find that the person sitting across the table is one of your supervisor's best friends. What are the chances that they will go to their friend, your boss or supervisor, and tell them what they just heard you say?

The sailors of World War II used a saying which was a direct rebuttal of participating in idle talk: "Loose Lips Sink Ships." Don't fall victim of your loose lips and sink your own ship.

**19.  Ms. Socialite: the MIA**

"She can never be found when you need her; I guess she's off visiting her friends again. I am about ready to buy her a subscription to Social Butterfly magazine." Have you experienced the frustration of confronting a problem with a customer, an account, a machine, or another work-related or business issue, and not being able to find a fellow employee when you really needed them? You know that they were at work because you saw them an hour earlier. Calling their extension several times has gotten no response. You have emailed them, left a voicemail, and an hour later you still haven't heard back from them. You really need them, what's up? They are often on another floor or in another department visiting with friends. They spend several hours every day bouncing from desk to desk or cube to cube. One thing is for sure, they are missing in action.

Bosses and supervisors value employees who are available when they are needed. If you are always away from your cubicle or workstation and no one knows where you are and how to contact you, it is safe to say that you are missing in action. It is very frustrating when someone you really need to speak with about a critical issue can't be found.

Think of how it must feel when you are the person who needs to be contacted and you don't return your calls or respond to your emails. Sure, you have work of your own to do just like everyone else. The key here is to be available. When you have to leave your workstation, tell someone where you are going and how they may get in touch with you and leave a phone number or extension where you may be reached.

This simple courtesy can win you some big rewards when your coworkers, supervisors, and bosses know that you can always be reached when needed as a resource. This is more than simple courtesy; it is also a good business practice as well. Solve the MIA problem: stay at your workstation as much as is expected and practical.

## 20.  Lazy Susan

"She never pulls her weight around here. About the heaviest weight she has ever carried is the two pound dumbbell she keeps on her desk." Workers not pulling their weight are a major factor in determining who will be laid off or terminated. When bosses consider who they should lay off, this will be one of their major considerations. Bosses can use layoffs to rid the company of lazy people if they so choose. Are you a lazy employee who doesn't carry your part of the load?

In the second chapter you read about getting into the boss's mind to develop an understanding of how he decides which employees to lay off. If you had been the boss and your company had reached the point where you were forced to lay off 21 employees in order for the company to survive, where would you begin? You would start by laying off the newest hires. Then the first question you would ask yourself is: "Who can I do without?" This question brings us back to this consideration: Who is and who is not pulling his or her weight around the company? You can be 100% certain that this question is among the first to come up when the discussion about layoffs begins.

You can do some things which will help to make your job essential. One of the most important things is to excel at being productive. Whether you like it or not or whether you agree with it or not, you are being judged by your productivity, or output. If you are producing and doing things which help the company, you are probably safe. On the other hand, if you are doing as little as possible and barely meet the minimum expectations for your job, you may be in trouble.

Ask yourself this question. "What can I begin doing today that will make me a much more productive employee?" Make a list of 10 things you could implement that would improve your chances of survival. Please note however, that even though you may be among the most productive people at your job you may still get the axe...if your entire department is laid off.

## 21. The Mirage

"He only works hard when I come around. Does he ever snap to attention? I'm afraid that one of these days he is going to hurt himself. I'm tempted to buy him a pair of binoculars so he can see me coming from a mile away." Almost everyone turns it up a notch or two and gets busy when he sees the boss coming toward his or her area. But some people carry this to the extreme edge of the envelope. They haven't accomplished anything meaningful for hours or days, but the moment the boss comes around they morph into the number one star employee. You know people who fit into this category. They are typically lazy employees. They try and get by with doing the minimum amount of work most of the time. But, let them hear their supervisor's voice and they snap into action and get busy. When the boss asks them how their work is going, they are the first to tell him how busy they have been.

"You can fool some of the people some of the time but you can't fool all of the people all of the time." You may have your boss fooled. He may honestly think that you are a star employee. But others know your work habits. Guess what, they talk. You have a certain reputation at work. You are perceived as someone who works or as someone who slacks. By the way, it does show up in your productivity. Your boss may not be as oblivious to your behavior as you think.

List five additional reasons why you need to keep your job. 1. Family. 2. Food. 3. Housing. 4. Monthly bills. 5. Car payment. 6. 7. 8. 9. 10. It may be that these will motivate you to get busy and work when the boss is not around.

## 22. Ms. Two-Faced

"She says one thing to my face and another behind my back. I wonder what she would look like if she pulled her second face off?" One of the worst things that can be said of a person is that they are "two-faced." Saying something to a person's face and then saying the very opposite behind their back is what we are talking about.

One major payoff comes with being "two-faced." The payoff is: lack of respect. One of the most important things that a person can carry with them is their reputation. If you are known as someone who says one thing to a person's face and then the opposite behind their back, your reputation is shot. I guarantee that most, if not all of them, assume that you do just the same with them...respect them to their faces, but talk about them behind their backs. People do not respect you.

The sharp ones are actually playing you and beating you at your own game. They show every sign that they respect you. They show respect with their words, their actions, and their deeds, but behind your back they talk about just how two-faced you are. You are being beaten at your own game. How does that feel?

Bosses aren't dummies. It is highly likely that your boss knows something about how two-faced you really are. When it comes to layoff time you may find yourself getting a pink slip, and your boss may play you in the process...telling you to your face how he hates to see you go...but laughing behind your back as soon as you walk out his door. You earned it, you got what you deserved, are you satisfied?

How can you overcome this problem? Start by being honest and above reproach in the way you treat people. Are you so insecure that you can't treat all people with respect? In your smugness, you may think that you are Mr. or Ms. Perfect and that no one lives up to your standards of perfection. You are kidding yourself. You have faults just like all the rest of us. Who do you think you are, God?

## 23.  The Tattler

"Hey boss, do you know what Stacey just...." In day-care centers, kindergartens, and schools across the world children often practice the art of tattling on other kids. Inherent within those children is something that makes them think it is their job to straighten out the other kids. They go to an authority figure that can make an immediate difference, their teacher, and tattle on Johnny or Janie. It makes them feel important. Though they don't know the meaning of the word, it makes them feel superior.

Fast forward 30 years. Some of you are still playing the kindergarten game of tattling. It is a wonder the boss doesn't set up a kiddy playground for some of his or her employees and supervisors. Come on, it's time you grew up. Your responsibility at work is to see that you get all your work done in an acceptable manner. Your job is not to tell the boss or your supervisor what, Kim, Brianna, Tom, Tierra, and Sam are doing. What do you think your supervisor or boss thinks about your tattling? If you are really brave and have a pretty thick skin, why not ask them? You will probably be in for the shock of your life. It will be the last time you find yourself tempted to tattle on one of your fellow employees. Oh, did I forget to mention that they are disgusted with your tattling as well? Tattling neither gains friends nor elevates you in your boss' opinion.

Need an action plan to help you stop tattling? Here it is, better be quick or you will miss it...stop tattling. If that went over your head, try promising yourself that you will eat a handful of prunes the next time you tattle and maybe that will work. If that sounds a little drastic or unappetizing, try denying yourself a shopping trip or round of golf. That may stop you.

Note: the following three categories are sometimes difficult to see in other people. They are tough because some of these behaviors take place only in the minds of those who practice them. Many times, all three will reside in the same person. Though they are internal, they do have definite external manifestations and negative results which can be devastating to relationships in the workplace. Typically, the more serious cases may only be resolved by seeking legitimate spiritual and or professional help. Consider this illegal trilogy.

## 24.  The Judge

"She must think she works here to judge everyone. She really needs to lighten-up. I wonder if she has a black robe hanging in her closet?" Being judgmental and hyper-critical of everyone can elevate your position on the layoff list. The judgmental person has risen to the pinnacle of bad attitudes. Since you are so perfect, you have set yourself up as the preeminent judge of all the other people with whom you work. While you could never get away with demanding it, nothing would please you more than if all your co-workers would bow down to you at the beginning and end of every shift and acknowledge your perfection. No doubt, many complaints have been lodged against you, and your boss knows of your outlandish judgmental behavior.

Have you checked to see how many genuine friends you have at work lately? One wonders if the "friends" you do have are actually your friends, or, are they your friends out of self-defense...so you won't take your wrath out on them.

Were you ever judged unfairly? Do you remember how it felt? Back off and cut yourself and others some slack. Who appointed you judge over anyone? Unless your answer is: "God," then you do not have a leg to stand on. Give it up. You will be a much happier person and you will be much easier to work alongside. If you will change your approach, other people may begin to warm up to you instead of re-senting your pompous and condescending attitude.

## 25. The Jury

"Don't confuse him with the facts, his mind is already made up, he finds the defendant guilty as charged." There are those who work among us who are like the members of a jury. Only this jury is seated in a kangaroo court. No mat-ter what a person does or says, they are pronounced guilty by Mr. or Ms. Jury member. This person always seems to be able to find guilt in everyone, in everyone but themselves. If you have one of these jury members in your company, you are very fortunate if they work in any department other than your own.

If you are this person, take heart, your day in court is coming. The jury of your peers will treat you exactly the same way you have been treating them..."I find the defen-dant guilty as charged." They will refuse to cut you any slack at all. Stop this jury nonsense. You and everyone else will be much better off.

## 26. The Executioner

"The guy is ruthless in the way he treats other people. He keeps this huge medieval-looking letter opener on his desk; I sure wish he would lose it." Some weird people get their kicks from stabbing people in the back. This self-ap-pointed executioner has the mistaken notion that it is his job to carry out the "death sentence." This individual will do ev-erything in his power to see that the "guilty" are punished. The guilty people in this crazy guy's world are the people he has determined are guilty and who deserve punishment. They are guilty only by his warped standards. His weapons of choice include backstabbing, hatred, slandering, lying, tattling, getting even, setting traps, and at least 100 other negative virtues he has in his repertoire.

Do you know someone who is constantly stabbing other people in the back? Their snide remarks, razor sharp tongue, hateful disposition, and many other charming ways are to be avoided at all costs. Some crazies like the idea of setting people up in situations that will produce guaranteed failure. This type of behavior is just short of criminal and is something which is despised by everyone who is unfortunate enough to be their victim. What ever happened to fairness, honor, and character?

Why do people do crazy things like this? No one but them would know for certain, but it sure looks like they engage in such behavior in order to gain some sort of advantage for themselves. They will get their comeuppance when the boss is looking for people they can do without, because they will be the one on the receiving end for a change.

Are you the "executioner" at your place of business? If this is your role, you are not making any friends where you work. You may need some professional help.

## 27.  Mr. Universe

"He is the most inconsiderate person I have ever had work for me. He must think the world revolves around him. Last Friday I was tempted to buy a gigantic trophy to put on his desk." Please, no trophies for this guy. Being considerate of other people is the right thing to do and will usually produce positive benefits. I am not saying that you have to be "Mr. Nice Guy," and let everyone run over you all the time. What I am saying is that it never hurts to be considerate of the needs and wants of the other people you work with. Being considerate at work is a virtue. Whether you know it or not, and whether you like it or not, the world does not really revolve around you. If you are a jerk at work, everyone knows it and they talk about you behind your back. It may come as a big surprise, but there are other people in the world who have rights too. You need to grow up and mature. If you abuse the people you work with, it has been noticed. If you are a person who always has to have his or her way, it has been noticed as well.

One-year-old babies are used to getting their way all the time. You are 25, 35, or 55 years old. It's time to stop being such a baby who whines and pouts when he or she doesn't get his or her way. Grow up. Who told you that you were the most important person in the world?

Make a list of 5-10 things you can do this week that will show other people that you are on your way to becoming a more considerate person. Put them into practice immediately and then make this a daily habit. You may be blown away by how nice people are treating you one month from today.

## 28.  Mr. Superiority

"He never helps out with other people's projects: he thinks he's just too good for everyone else." Are you someone who is always helping other people with their projects at work? Have you ever been in a situation where you needed another person's help and were denied because they were too busy to offer help? One of the most frustrating things you can possibly experience is the scenario outlined above. You bust your buns to help someone who is in a jam and they not only refuse to return the favor, they act as though you have insulted them for even asking for their help. It makes you say something like: "That's the last time I will ever do anything to help him."

One of the most positive ways you can impact your boss' opinion is to help other people who are in a tight spot. If you gladly consent to assist someone, enable them to look good, and help the company in the process, you have done something very worthwhile.

However, you have to know where to draw the line when it comes to helping people. If you are not careful, you may end up doing a lot of peoples work for them. Volunteer to "help" someone, don't volunteer to do someone's work for them. Remember, any time you spend helping another person is time you are spending away from your own work. You have to know when to say "No," in order to protect yourself and your time.

Avoid allowing yourself to be seen as some "good ole Sam or Sally," the person that another can dump their projects on and expect you to finish them while they take a break or chat on the phone. One way to break this habit if you have already fallen into this trap is to set limits and tell the other person. "I will gladly help you with your project as long as we work on it together." The minute they excuse themselves to go and do something else is the minute when you stop working on their project and go back to working on your own projects.

The next time someone asks for your help tell them up front, "Mark, I'll be happy to help you, but I will need you to return the favor next week when I work on the Anderson project." If Mark agrees to accept your help and he agrees to help you on your project next week that's great. Be sure and collect the favor and ask him to help you. If next week comes and he says he is too busy, you may need to say something like: "Mark, last week when I helped you work on the Goldberg project you said you would help me on the Anderson project. I have been counting on your help and need to know when you will be able to help me." Mark may have forgotten and may respond by assisting you immediately. He may say that he is at a critical point and that he can't stop right now but will be available in one hour. Finally, he may have never intended to help you and he just said that to get you to help him. At any rate, you can make your decision about helping Mark in his future endeavors based upon what you want to do.

How do I change my ways if I'm the guy who never helps anybody? Simple, you can solve that problem tomorrow. Find someone who is struggling with a project and offer your help. I said help, not take over.

Others may reject your offers to help the first few times you offer to help. They may reject your offers simply because they are stunned or they may fear that you have an ulterior motive. Keep offering, but not in a condescending manner. Once people know your offers are sincere they will be wondering what book you have been reading. Let them read your copy...it may help them too.

## 29. The Text Berry

"All I ever get is a Busy Signal: she takes her phone off the hook and spends most of her time on her text berry." Do you remember the days when cell phones and text messages didn't rule people's lives? It seems that every person in America has their own phone and they are not hesitant to use them at work. I have seen a few people who have two or three different phones. Cell use is quickly becoming one of the most annoying problems at work. Have you ever been in the middle of an important conversation when the person you are talking with has to stop to take a call on their cell? They spend the next ten minutes talking about what to have for dinner and catch up on the latest news about Aunt Matilda's ingrown toenail. Meanwhile, you wait. You are trapped; it's almost like you are being held hostage while you are forced to hear one side of a conversation which you don't really care to hear. Not only do people receive cell calls, two of the other biggest offenders are those of sending and receiving text and picture messages. Some people's thumbs will probably fall off before they reach age 40. You may be able to get a laugh out of this one if you feign thumb sprain. Wrap them both in gauze while at lunch one day and see if you can get a laugh or two. This would be especially fitting if you are the one who has a problem with your text berry.

When it comes to making personal calls on company time, each company has their own set of guidelines. Check with your supervisor or HR department to gain a clear understanding of your company's rules governing cell phone use. Abide by them. The job you save may be your own. How do I cut back on cell and text usage? Simple. Leave it in your car, leave it at home, throw it away, or smash it. I don't care what you do; just put it where it can't get you in trouble at work.

## 30. Ms. Gossip

"I hope her last name is "Miller," she's the owner of the gossip and rumor mills around here." Do you have someone in your workplace whose major contribution to work is that they are always talking about others? They may as well put a sign on their desk that says "rumor mill." This person is not your friend. If they spread rumors about everybody else in the office, it doesn't take a genius to guess what they say about you when you are not there.

Being known as the one who is always spreading rumors does not ingratiate one to his or her boss. Just wait until the boss gets wind of a rumor which Mr. or Ms. Rumor Control started about him or her. The boss might just be temped to spread a rumor of his own. There once was an old saying which went something like this: "If you can't say something good about someone, don't say anything at all." If you are the chief grinder at the rumor mill at your place of employment, stop before someone pays you back.

## 31. The Favor Granter

"All I ever hear about her is that she provides 'favors' to some of the guys from the office. I hear that he's the go-to guy if someone wants to buy drugs." It is very unfortunate, but the reason some people are able to keep their jobs has nothing to do with their work. The only reasons they stay on with the company are the "favors" they provide the boss or others within the company. These could be "favors" of a pharmacological, sexual, monetary, or other nature. If someone chooses to engage in these types of behaviors, they should go ahead and have someone paint a target on their back because when they are caught by the right person they will be fired.

Where is common decency and dignity in this equation? It is non-existent. If the only reason someone is able to keep a job is some "favor" they can supply the boss or someone else in the company, they are on the lowest rung of the ladder. Many at work have little or no respect for them.

A person who is engaged in "favor" granting is like a plastic bottle or aluminum soda can; once the contents are poured out, the container is either tossed away or recycled. If you are supplying "favors", you are accomplishing only one thing, being used. When those who are using you are through with you, you will be tossed aside, laid off, or terminated. It will be much easier for the boss if you are no longer there because you could provide evidence against him or her. If you are involved in immoral or illegal practices with your boss, both of you are treading on thin ice. Unless the boss is also the business owner, he could be terminated right alongside you.

One of the quickest ways to get your layoff or termination ticket punched is to exchange "favors" for your job. Stop being a dope. Stop being used. Stop supplying, and if you're stopping elicits a threat from the boss, you may present him with a choice. Tell him that you have decided to stop and that he will either have to leave you alone or he will go down with you. Don't make an idle threat. Be fully prepared to take this issue over his head or to the police if necessary. Be careful, this can get you fired or worse.

### 32. Mr. Contraband

"This guy is always on the borderline of being illegal." This catch-all term is used to indicate a variety of things which are not allowed or tolerated at your workplace. Most violations will result in either a layoff or an immediate termination. Since your company or business will have policies governing each of the following, it is not possible to say what will happen in every situation. You should be aware that each of these and some others are treated very seriously and may result in an immediate layoff or termination. These offenses include:

- all drug use, including refusal to take a drug test
- alcohol consumption on the job
- bringing firearms, weapons, or explosives to work
- workplace violence, fighting or inflicting bodily harm upon another person
- threatening a customer or employee
- offensive behavior, displaying offensive materials
- extreme anger, rage
- deliberate property damage
- other

## 33. Mr. Put-Down

Two supervisors were talking and one said: "You wouldn't believe what that guy said to me a couple of years ago." One of the surest ways to be targeted for a layoff is to put other people down. This is especially true when it comes to putting down your boss, supervisor, manager, or business owner. Many bosses have superb memories. If they hear you have been criticizing them, another boss, or another employee, you could face some serious consequences. Some bosses are vindictive, some like to make you pay for the things you said or did, and some bosses don't get mad, they get even. You don't want to have to work for a boss who is out to get you for something you said. What you say to a co-worker about your boss could come back to haunt you later.

A good practice is that of being judicious in what you say to everyone where you work. You never know when your words might be used against you. Words stick, and once they are spoken, words cannot be recalled.

One man had publicly criticized another man extremely unfairly and harshly. After a few months, the critic acknowledged his mistake and decided that he would apologize. He approached the man whom he had criticized severely, and asked for his forgiveness. The man was shocked at the apology. He excused himself and returned a moment later carrying a pillow. He asked his critic to follow him to his office window and he promptly shook the feathery contents of the pillow into the wind outside his window. Puzzled, his critic asked: "Why did you do that?" The man who had been unfairly criticized said: "I will accept your apology if you will go and retrieve all the feathers that came out of this pillow." His critic responded: "Why, that would be impossible." The offended man said: "Your words of criticism have been scattered far and wide and the damage can never be undone." Watch the words you speak; they will be carried like feathers upon the wind.

How do I stop this behavior and prevent it from getting me fired? Zip it. Don't say anything to or about your boss that you don't want remembered. If you have said some things in the past that you regret saying to your boss, what would happen if you went to him with an honest heart-felt apology?

## Do the Exact Opposite of These 33 Things

You get the picture. You can virtually layoff proof your job by doing the exact opposite of any one or any combination of these 33 things. And the list goes on. Examine your specific job to discover other behaviors that would apply to your job specifically. If you found that you have been doing any of these things then…STOP…doing them immediately. Stopping may be tough, but the job you save may be your own. In fact, stopping them may prevent your name from even being considered as an addition to the boss's layoff list. The caricatures enabled us to see just how foolish some these behaviors appear to your boss and other employees. Hopefully, they also enabled you to see how they can negatively impact your own job and the jobs of other people as well. Now you know why some bosses decide that their companies can do without certain employees.

An experienced military person once said: "When standing in formation, don't do anything that would cause you to be noticed." To keep your job, don't get yourself noticed doing any of the 33 things listed above. (Don't tell any-body, but refraining from these negative practices works well at home with your spouse and kids as well.)

**The Takeaway**

The purpose of this chapter was to enable you to iden-tify behaviors that invite layoffs or terminations. By identify-ing them, you are now one step closer to layoff proofing yourself and your job. Were you able to see yourself in any of the 33 caricatures? If you made an honest attempt and were able to see yourself in one or more of them, you have placed yourself in a position to be able to change your habits, actions, attitudes, practices, and behaviors as they relate to your job. The quicker you begin making the neces-sary adjustments and the more obvious these adjustments become to your boss, the quicker you can begin layoff proofing yourself and your job.

The first reaction some have when reading the 33 cari-catures is their feeling that a lot of other people are in need of changes. Many never see the need for changes in their own lives or behaviors. The lack of a vision to begin mak-ing necessary changes makes layoff proofing oneself dif-ficult, if not impossible. Why, because they get stuck in com-placency, become myopic, refuse to see their own flaws, and deny the fact that they are the person who needs to change the most.

**Be Painfully Honest**

Now would be a good time for you to be totally hon-est with yourself and identify changes you can make that can help you keep your job. Do any of the 33 behaviors need immediate attention as they relate to you and your job? Write the most significant changes you need to make in the following blanks. List them in order of importance and begin changing the most important one immediately. After the first issue has been resolved, work on the next one, and the next, until you have finished your list.

Changes I would like to make:

1.

2.

3.

4.

5.

Consider asking a close and trusted friend at work to look at your list and give their honest critique of your performance and behavior at work. Whether you choose to make improvements yourself or ask a friend for help, make the changes you need to make.

The next few chapters are designed to enable you to take the other major steps you need in order to layoff proof yourself entirely. You will be challenged to confront and to change various aspects of your thinking, decision-making, and behavior. Once you have made significant strides toward making the changes that you deem necessary, you will have successfully layoff proofed yourself, and ostensibly, your job as well.

Some may have reached such a level of discomfort that they may choose to stop reading this book at this point. At least take the following principle with you: Treat people the way you wish to be treated.

If you desire respect, treat people with respect. If you desire honesty and truth, be honest and truthful. If you desire friendship and acceptance, give friendship and acceptance. If you desire to be rewarded for the work you perform, make sure that what you do is worthy of the kinds of rewards you expect to receive. In essence, you will receive what you give to other people.

Now, consider positive steps you may take to save your job.

# Chapter 5
# Job-Saving Steps You Can Take

A relief pitcher is usually brought into a baseball game in order to salvage a bad situation. The pitcher ahead of him may have given up one or more runs, loaded the bases, and placed the outcome of the game in jeopardy. In addition to saving the game, a highly-skilled relief pitcher can make the difference between a team's having just an average season and playing in the World Series.

Some of you would love to have the luxury of having a skilled specialist come in, relieve you, and save your job. The bad news is that it is not going to happen. The good news is that you have the freedom to develop your own personal strategy that can help you avoid a potential layoff. You may begin anywhere you wish.

The bottom line is that there are highly-effective job-saving steps available for you to take. The desired outcome for your personal job situation is that you can clearly define what you want to accomplish and then make it happen. You may do many things to demonstrate to your superiors that you are an employee that they need to keep. Listen to the words of that experienced military person again. "When standing in formation, don't do anything that would cause you to be noticed." Did you notice that he framed his words in a negative context? As someone attempting to make changes that will enable you to layoff proof yourself and your job, you do need to be noticed. You need for your boss to notice you and notice the improvements you are making.

## Being Noticed Isn't All Bad

Remove the negative behaviors and replace them with the positive changes you are making. You want to be noticed when it comes to your new work-ethic, attitude, thinking, behavior, habits, skills, decision-making, and performance at work. You want to be noticed when it comes to your new level of commitment to begin making a more significant contribution to your company.

There are definite steps you may take that will cause you be noticed. Depending upon how effective you become in implementing them, they can help you keep your job. Again, there are no guarantees, but by doing the 25 things listed below, you may greatly increase your chances of keeping your job should layoffs begin making the rounds in your company.

Do you remember my caution: Extremely Heavy Content Ahead? Here is the second installment. Heavy content lies ahead. But there are major differences...all of these are positive things you are encouraged to begin implementing immediately.

The following steps are designed to give you a head start as you begin to think about ways to make significant changes in your work life. You would be advised not to take the following steps lightly. In fact, you may wish to consider making a copy of the following steps and placing them in a prominent place in your home or at work.

## 25 Steps to Save your Job

1. Work hard and work smart; both will pay off.
2. Create a list of things you can do that will make you more valuable to your company.
3. Do everything in your power to get along with your boss and everyone else.
4. Be a team player and play by company rules.
5. Do things that will enable you to stand out from the crowd.
6. Arrive for work early and stay until your shift ends.

7. Be the first to volunteer to work overtime if asked to finish a project.

8. Get your boss' permission to learn unique computer or other skills that no one else has and put them to work in your company immediately.

9. Keep a private log of your accomplishments...in case you need to show your boss, and then only if it is needed. Use your own better judgment here.

10. Give a full day's work for a full day's pay.

11. Be fair-minded to all and loyal to your job.

12. Be honest and above reproach in all things.

13. Be easily approachable by everyone.

14. Really know your stuff: gain a mastery over your assigned job.

15. Always, always, always make your boss look good. He will love it and you may share in the benefits.

16. Be balanced and keep your cool in as many situations as possible.

17. Treat others with the same courtesy and decency you expect from them.

18. Be an exemplary employee, the kind your boss could point out to a new employee and say: "If you want to know how to succeed around here, be just like him or her."

19. Look for ways to offer legitimate compliments and praise to other workers or managers. Dale Carnegie once wrote a book about winning friends and influencing people. You can put his methods to work for you.

20. Volunteer for extra or tough assignments that no one else will tackle.

21. Build up your fellow employees. Everyone would love to hear a positive and encouraging word now and then.

22. Acknowledge another person's good idea, their new way of performing a task, or their success in handling a tough situation.

23. Offer to lend a helping hand when you see someone struggling with a difficult assignment.

24. Respect other people and their right to have their own opinions even when they differ from yours.

25. Always remember, it's never wrong to do the right thing.

26. And on it goes; you can add your own steps here.

The bottom line is that you clearly define what you want to accomplish and then make it happen. Produce measurable results by doings things that are both positive and tangible in order to demonstrate to your superiors that you are an employee that they need to keep.

You get the picture. You can virtually layoff proof yourself and your job by doing these 25 things. If you have already been doing any of these positive things, CONTINUE doing them and any others you might add.

**Your Job is a Privilege, Not a Right**

This concept may come as a surprise for some and it may burst the bubbles of a few others. It could wreak havoc with those who have been educated in the "self-esteem" based educational system of many of today's public schools. The principle is this: Your job is a privilege, not a right.

You may have never thought of it like this before, and it may come as a surprise to you, but your boss does not have to let you work for him or for his company. You have been extended the opportunity to work there because: you possess a talent, a skill-set, knowledge, or an ability which is valuable to your business or company.

Unfortunately, if you come to the place where you no longer benefit the company, you will no longer be needed… it's that simple. If you become less productive and someone comes along who can do more for the company than you, you may be out of a job. Look at the way professional sports teams treat their former stars and legends of past seasons. They trade them. Not many employees are allowed to stay around beyond their usefulness to the company.

This is not to suggest that you should become paranoid about your job; that will only make you miserable. However, avoid having the "I'm God's gift to this company," attitude. No one likes arrogance and that type of pride. Your fellow employees, your supervisor, your boss, the CEO, and not even God himself likes arrogance and improper pride. The Scriptures say: "There are six things the LORD hates, seven that are detestable to him: haughty eyes, a lying tongue, hands that shed innocent blood, a heart that devises wicked schemes, feet that are quick to rush into evil, a false witness who pours out lies and a man who stirs up dissension among brothers" Proverbs 6:16-19 (NIV).

Translated to the workplace it means: "The boss hates arrogance, a liar, a troublemaker, someone who is always plotting evil, someone who is always quick to do evil, someone who lies to get others in trouble, and a person who is himself a troublemaker."

Economic times are tough and may even get tougher. Let's take a positive look at how a person can set himself up in a job that doesn't seem like its work at all.

# Chapter 6
# From Hope to Hopelessness and Back Again

He was a poor boy with a dream, growing up along-side the unpaved back roads of rural Texas. No one ever dreamed he would become a celebrity one day. He came from a large family and his dad was a rancher for as long as anyone could remember. As far as everyone was concerned, the boy's life was mapped out the day he was born...he would be a rancher like his dad, his granddad, and his great granddad before him.

His name was Joseph and he was building a dream. One summer he collected and sold aluminum cans he found alongside the road. He used the money to buy his family a radio. Joseph dreamed of leaving the ranch one day and traveling to distant cities he had only heard of on the radio or in his classes at school. He dreamed of having a family of his own and of owning his very own car one day. One of his dreams involved traveling to St Louis to watch his favorite baseball team, the Cardinals, play.

Joseph was the youngest child in the family and would tell his older brothers his dreams. They would laugh at him and aggravate him, saying: "Joe, you will never leave this ranch and amount to anything. Your dreams are silly; all you are is a good-for-nothing 'Dreamer' who will stay here and work for us forever." His brothers' words hurt Joe to the core of his being, but he refused to allow them to crush his spirit or kill his dream of becoming something one day.

His family was proud of their radio. Late in the evenings on those blistering hot Texas days when the work was finished and the livestock fed and watered, the family would gather around the radio and listen to KMOX from St. Louis, Missouri. Joe loved to listen for the Cardinals to hit home runs. Little did he know that he had a future and that he would one day live that dream himself.

Joe was a good kid and a hard worker who never complained. He was good at throwing rocks. Of necessity he learned that skill as a youngster when his dad would ask him to help clear a field for planting. He was good. He could hit a fence post with almost every throw from 20 yards away. Jake, Joe's dad, recognized his son's potential and bought him a baseball and glove. That summer they would often play catch until the radio broadcast started.

By the next summer the entire family joined in the fun and played baseball in the front yard almost every evening until dark. Some of the neighbors started joining in and before the summer ended, they had enough people to field two complete baseball teams. Each night they would choose up sides and everybody who wanted to play got to play. Girls, boys, old, and young enjoyed the game. They always kept the score, but they were much more concerned with having fun than who won the nightly games. After the sun went down and the last out was had, they would all join together on the front porch for his mother Rachael's lemonade and cookies.

By the third summer, news of the games traveled far and wide. Joe's skills had so developed that even a couple of coaches came by to watch him play. He had refined a pretty good complement of pitches; throwing all those rocks had finally come in handy. When small kids would come up to bat, Joe would throw underhanded and encourage them to hit the ball. If a strapping young teen or a grown man wanted to challenge Joe's arm, he would wind up and send a rocket across the plate and strike them out almost every time.

By now, Jake and Rachel owned a car. For the entire year leading up to Joe's 16th birthday they saved for a family vacation. With the help of the high school coach, the entire family went to St. Louis to attend their first major league baseball game. And yes, one of the Cardinals belted one over the wall to win the game. The coach even arranged for the family to get to meet some of the players after the game was over. By now his brothers' jealousy had increased and they began to disrespect Joe more than ever.

Joe shrugged them off and dealt with them the best way he knew how; he excelled in baseball. Throughout high school he was scouted by several large colleges with excellent baseball programs. More than one big-time college coach who came to his house on a recruiting visit actually ended up joining in a friendly game of baseball and drank lemonade on Rachel's front porch. Joe settled on the University of Texas.

When it came time for Joe to leave for the university, his brothers were happy for him to leave home. In their final act of disrespect, they created lame excuses to avoid having to spend much time at his going away party. The love and family values modeled by his parents taught him and his siblings how to relate to people, although his brothers hadn't learned that lesson when it came to their brother Joe. All was not lost, his parents' sincere faith in God, modeled on a daily basis, taught him how to have a strong relationship with the Lord.

Joe cried when he left, but he was ready to begin living his dream. He excelled both academically and athletically in college. His strong work-ethic had taught him self discipline. Life was good. Joe was watched by major-league scouts from the first day he suited up for a college game. He did not disappoint them. No less than a dozen major league teams expressed interest in having him play for them. His heart was in St. Louis.

After he played his rookie year, a reporter asked him how he liked playing ball for his beloved Cardinals. Joe said: "I'm living the dream." His rookie season saw him marry his high school and college sweetheart, Jan. They were madly in love and deeply committed to one another and their marriage. Jan was the perfect wife. Not only was she supportive of Joe's baseball career, she was an entrepreneur who developed a very successful computer programming career of her own.

The crowning point of Joe's baseball career came when he pitched and helped his team win the World Series. The same reporter asked him if he thought all the hard work had been worth it. Joe said: "I never worked one day at baseball in my life, I'm living the dream."

Living the dream suddenly turned into a living nightmare the next season when Joe suffered an injury that benched him from pitching. He had the requisite shoulder surgery and spent months in rehab in an attempt to be ready for the next season. Frustration set in. Despair and despondency became constant companions. He desperately missed the game and pinned his baseball hopes on being able to join the pitching rotation the next season. Jan, and Joe's dad and mother were very supportive and encouraging.

Spring training came and baseball life began moving again. He worked out with the team and began pitching in rotation in the spring games. Joe, and everyone else, knew that his pitches didn't have the snap they once had. As the season started he was placed in the rotation and won several games, but he lost many more than he used to. Finally, his manager assigned him a slot as a relief pitcher. One month later he was sent down to the minors. Joe felt like his career was over, and it was. He was later released from the team. His dream was shattered.

For the first time in his life he was unemployed. He had once lived the dream but now his dream had ended. He spent the next several months going in and out of depression, moping, wallowing in self-pity, and feeling sorry for himself. What hurt him the most was the fact that he had been to the top of his career and now he was unemployed.

He had been laid off from the job he loved. The only difference between him and the guys who had been laid off down at the factory was that he was receiving a meager baseball retirement check and they weren't.

One day Joe had been praying, reading his Bible, reflecting, feeling like a failure, and crying when he suddenly had the urge to get up and get over his pity-party. He felt as though the Lord had spoken to him and made him realize that it was time for him to get on with the rest of his life. He ran, embraced Jan, told her he loved her and what he had just experienced, and they talked for hours. Together, they made the decision to move back to Texas where he had many contacts. After their move he began calling some of his old friends and front yard baseball teammates. Within a month he had decided that he would begin raising cattle and start ranching. There was one major difference however; this time he would be the owner, not just a rancher's kid. Then the bubble burst again when he and Jan were unable to borrow enough money to buy the small ranch and a few pieces of farm equipment to get them started.

After a month of doing nothing, Joe felt like a total failure. He had bottomed out emotionally, financially, and spiritually. The economy was so bad that neither he nor Jan could find work in their small Texas town. He decided to pass his time by helping his old high school coach with spring practice. Jan finally landed a job as a computer programmer at a bank 20 miles from where they lived. They clung to one another for emotional support and found a friendly church where they could worship and receive spiritual support.

Today Joe is finally employed, well, sort-of employed. He and Jan were able to buy the same property he grew up on, and they are making their living by ranching. He feels as though he has come full-circle. He had left ranching to play baseball and now he had left baseball to do ranching. He, Jan, and their new daughter are happy. After the first year Joe realized that he missed baseball immensely, but he was surprised to realize that he was enjoying ranching just about as much.

Living the dream is becoming a reality once again. He now knows that he has succeeded because he has the right sense of priorities in his life. His faith, family, and ranching, is what keeps him going. He and Jan are teaching their daughter to bow her head and give God thanks for her blessings. Joe and Jan are happy because they have discovered many of the secrets to a happy life. They have a renewed sense of hope, for when he celebrated his birthday all his brothers came over and surprised him with a birthday cake. Their long-term goal is to buy the property adjacent to the land they already own.

## How to Never Work Again

Joe still says that he never worked a day in his life. He is one of those rare individuals who were able to make the most out of life's ever-changing situations. A purist at heart, he found something he absolutely loved to do and turned it into a career. Talk about fun; he was paid to do what he loved doing. He followed his dream.

Your life and mine may not be quite as glamorous as Joe's. Life in the factory, in a cubicle, or in the corporate board room may not be as exciting as life on the major-league baseball diamond. Regardless of what you are doing now, Joe's story can teach us some things that will help us gain a new perspective about our jobs. I like his thinking about how he never had to work at baseball or ranching a day in his life. So much of success goes back to attitude, outlook, and perspective.

## Work is a Joy When your Heart is in Your Job!

If you are fortunate enough to have identified your passion, and are able to work in a job or vocation you are passionate about, your work will never seem like work. Your heart will be in your work and your work will be a joy. You will find that you go to work with a sense of excitement, purpose, and fulfillment. Job performance, morale, motivation, raises, and promotions will become automatic. Work will never seem like work if your heart is in what you do, and you:

- Identify and work within the area of your passion
- Live your dream
- Enjoy what you do
- Excel at what you do
- Develop right priorities

How does a person identify his or her passion? Here is a simple test. What do you enjoy doing more than anything else in the entire world? If you were age 35, already had all the money you needed and no longer needed to work, what would you do with your time? What motivates you to get up early and stay up late? What brings you the greatest feelings of satisfaction, accomplishment, fulfillment, and pride? If you could wake up tomorrow morning and do anything you wanted to do, what would you do? What have other people suggested you should consider doing? Your answers to these questions reveal a lot about your passion. Your passion is something you would do without being paid. Your passion is something that you look forward to more than anything else. Your passion is that which excites you, captures your attention, invigorates you, motivates you, and gives you a genuine sense of fulfillment and accomplishment. Your passion is something that would get you up early and keep you up late.

What are you good at doing? That may or may not be your passion. It is possible to be highly successful in a particular job or vocation but not enjoy your work. Take time to reflect on your passion and follow your heart. Ask for input from those who know you best. Seek to identify your passion, and if you choose to do so, move toward developing a career in that area. If you are unable to develop it into a career, consider volunteering or working one day per week in that area. Many people have found a wonderful sense of fulfillment by doing exactly that. Not everyone can afford to quit their job, and spend the rest of their life following their dream or their passion. However, just knowing that every Thursday night or every Saturday morning you will be spending time doing something you are really passionate about may make your primary job much more palatable. You only get to go around once in this life, so you may as well enjoy doing what you do for the rest of your life on earth. "For I know the plans I have for you, declares the Lord, plans to prosper you and not to harm you, plans to give you hope and a future" Jeremiah 29:11 (NIV).

Work can be both a curse and a blessing. It has been both to me. I, along with many others, have discovered that work becomes what we want it to be. I have had jobs that I hated and jobs that I loved. Chances are that you could probably say the same thing about your career history.

Many readers are facing probable layoffs. Other readers have already experienced a layoff and are now living in the aftermath. Still others are desperately searching for work, any type of work. They would take any job at this point in the layoff-ridden economy we are experiencing. I recently read of one 90 plus year-old-man who is now working for $10 per hour after losing his life's savings of $700,000 in an investment scam. This may be a harbinger of tough times ahead.

Would you like to have advance notice if a layoff was coming to your company? There are definite warning signs that often precede layoffs.

# Chapter 7
# Warning Signs That Predict Layoffs

How empowering would it be for you to have advance knowledge that a layoff was coming to your company before it was announced? That advance knowledge would enable you to begin your job search and possibly secure another job before being laid off. Learning to recognize layoff warning signs can become a valuable tool to have in your portfolio. This chapter is designed to enable you to spot the warning signs that precede layoffs before they are implemented. An accurate understanding and interpretation of these warning signs may buy you some much-needed time on your job. In a topsy-turvy economy, the time it buys may only be a few weeks to a few months. Thankfully, you could use that time, however brief, to your advantage. You may be able to spot the layoff coming while it is still on the horizon, before it slams ashore like a devastating hurricane.

If you get sick and go to your family doctor for treatment, the first thing she does is to identify your symptoms. Once she knows your symptoms, she can then diagnose your illness. Businesses often exhibit symptoms of sicknesses as well. Their symptoms can serve as warning signs that they are facing problems ahead. Those symptoms may signal that a business is facing a layoff, a buyout, or an impending closing. If you are able to observe the warning signs or symptoms experienced by your company, you may be able to avoid a painful outcome by knowing when to stay on board or when to begin looking for another job.

It is true that someone should not practice medicine without a license. Neither should someone practice diagnosing a business' problems without having all the facts, knowledge, and experience that would qualify one to make an accurate prediction. Therefore, be very cautious as you interpret these warning signs. **Resist the temptation to read into your company's situation things that are not really there.** Consider the first and second examples for instance. In today's economy almost every business is experiencing a reduction in output because of the recession. Likewise, almost every company's stock is down because the stock market sustained tremendous losses in late 2008 and early 2009. You may recognize some of the warning signs immediately. However, they do not automatically imply that your company is ready to implement layoffs or is getting ready to close. The signs you recognize may mean that your business's CEO, owner, board of directors, home office, or manager is attempting to prevent the possibility of layoffs or closing the business.

Avoid paranoia as you look for signs that things are changing. Interpret the signs only as they apply to your company. Not every sign will apply to each and every individual company's situation. However, should you begin noticing that your company is doing several of the following; you may want to weigh your options about applying for another job.

Should you read this list and notice that your company has already experienced several of these changes, what should you do? Ask questions of your CEO, owner, or supervisor. Since most companies are taking many measures to cut back on expenses and save money; by taking drastic measures like some of those listed below, your company may be attempting to save your job.

Now, if you are confident that your company is planning a layoff or is planning to close, schedule an appointment with your boss and discuss your thoughts with him or her. They may be able to give you a heads-up. However, it is possible that your boss knows what is coming, but is forbidden to discuss it until a public announcement is made.

## Should I Be Afraid?

This chapter is not about fear, nor is it my goal to scare anyone. That said, it does offer some sobering insights into the realities of the way business is conducted in today's economy.

As you consider the following list of warning signs, there are two very important things to remember. First, most of these warning signs are not stand-alone indicators that can predict guaranteed layoffs, terminations, or closures in your company's future. Don't base your information on just one or two warning signs. Your understanding and prediction of a coming layoff would be much more accurate if your company begins linking significant groups of the following warning signs together.

Second, many of these signs are general in nature. To know what is really happening in your company, you will need to interpret the signs that are specific to your company.

Predicting a layoff can be more difficult than predicting which team will become the national champions of your favorite sport. Why? Because there are simply too many variables involved. Too many times to count, football, baseball, and basketball teams have been ready to declare their games lost, when in the closing seconds, they either scored a touchdown, hit a home run, or hit a three point shot from half court to secure a come-from-behind victory. The only sure predictions that can be made about the ultimate outcomes of sporting events and layoffs, terminations, and closures are that ultimately they are almost impossible to predict with 100% accuracy. There are simply too many variables.

Join me in considering the following predictors of coming layoffs.

## Warning Signs That Predict Layoffs
### 1.   Production begins to plummet

While almost every company's production is down, you observe that your company is not producing the same amount of product or goods and services it was one month ago. This becomes noticeable when you begin finishing your work an hour or two earlier each day, when sales begin to drop, or you notice that work in general has begun slowing down. If this begins happening in your workplace, begin looking for other corresponding signs. Something may be in the works and you may be able to determine what it is.

### 2.   Stock values begin to plummet

Due to the fact that almost every stock across the board experienced large hits in 2008 and early 2009, this category may be harder to determine than it would have during better economic times. That said, should you notice a precipitous drop in your company's stock, this could be a foreboding warning that something is in the making. Begin looking for additional signs that say changes are coming to your workplace.

### 3.   Company institutes a hiring freeze

If your company typically hires a constant stream of new employees but suddenly stops, you know that something is up. Though this single sign alone can't possibly tell you what is happening, a hiring freeze usually signals the fact that money is tight and that the company is taking measures to stay in business. This warning sign could be a precursor of future actions to come. As with so many other things, it will depend greatly upon the economy.

### 4.   Incoming orders slow to a trickle

Lack of incoming orders signals that your business is not doing well. It also signals that the customers or clients who bought products or services from your company are not doing well. Watch this one closely, for your company is in business to make money and customers and clients are the people who generate your company's cash flow. If the cash stops flowing, some drastic steps may have to be taken.

**5.    Outgoing shipments slow to a trickle**

Should you notice that outgoing shipments suddenly drop off, you must surmise that something is up. Have they been dropping steadily over the past few months or did they drop suddenly? Draw your own conclusions but watch this one closely. Your company may be on the verge of implementing a mass layoff or it could be on the verge of going under. Unless orders and shipments increase, cuts will have to be made.

**6.    Raw materials, stockpiles, or retail stocks dwindle**

Should you be alarmed if you notice that normal stockpiles of raw materials are allowed to dwindle to almost nothing? Should you be frightened if you notice that store shelves are becoming empty? Answer these two questions: What is your company going to sell if the shelves are becoming empty? What will it manufacture if it eliminates the raw materials that are used to manufacture the products? This looks like a sure sign that something big is coming. You need to begin asking a lot of questions, and getting your résumé or application submitted to other companies.

**7.    Employee hours are trimmed back**

Many retail stores and factories trim back during lean times. Just because they are doing it again during a tough economy may mean nothing or it could mean a lot more that it usually does. If the cutbacks are like all the previous ones, it may mean little at all. If the cutbacks are much more drastic, there may be reason for concern. Watch this sign and pay close attention to see if others are able to be linked to it.

**8.    Managers are laid off or fired**

"Well we finally got rid of Jack; I've wanted to see him go for a couple of years now." Jack's departure could be a signal that other managers or supervisors are soon to follow. Watch this one closely. Pay close attention to whether

Jack's position is filled or left vacant. When personnel begin being picked off it could be a sign that more firings or lay-offs are on the way. Those who may be especially vulnerable are those who have a long tenure, are getting up in years, or are making larger than average salaries.

**9.    Other employees are laid off or fired**

Pay close attention to whether hourly employees' positions are being filled or left vacant. Never hesitate to talk with your supervisor about what is happening and whether you or your work group will be affected. What you observe happening in the company and how your supervisor responds to your questions will tell you some very important things about what to expect in the future.

**10.    Your industry impacted by recession**

Industries that have sustained terrible hits include: automotive, banking, construction, health care, investments, real estate, transportation, and retail, to name a few. These industries will one day regain their viability regardless of the depth of a recession or future depression within America. The industry will remain, but will the particular branch, agency, dealership, or office you work in be able to survive? No one knows for sure. If you are in one of these or a similar industry you may wish to do some evaluating to see whether this is what you want to continue doing or whether now is the time to consider changing careers.

**11.    Company has huge amounts of debt**

If you know for a fact that your company is distressed with an overwhelming amount of debt there may be need for concern. Debt is the giant wrecking ball of industry and business. It can level the biggest and best of them all the way down to the smallest. This may be indicative of a closing rather than a mass layoff. In this case, closure is tantamount to bankruptcy. How could someone know whether his company was experiencing great debt? Have you noticed formidable outlays of monies for renovations, large equipment purchases, or other recent purchases? Can companies work themselves out of debt and survive recession? Yes, they can and yes, they have. Not all of them can be so blessed however.

**12. Expense accounts are cut back or scaled back**

This may be no more than a good controller stepping up and doing his job, that of controlling the purse strings. Taken alone, this sign probably means little more than that. Couple this with several others and you may have need for concern.

**13. Company contracts with an efficiency expert to analyze worker output**

This is a sure sign, if not a guaranteed predictor, that layoffs or terminations are coming. If an outside firm is contracted to do a "study" of your workplace and workforce, you can bank on the fact that big changes are in the offing for someone. No matter what they tell you, the reason for this "study" is to be able to justify which positions can be eliminated. If they show up at your place of work, some employees need to begin getting their bags packed because some will wake up one day and no longer have a job. Does this mean that you will lose your job? No, it's not necessarily you who will lose your job, but chances are high that someone will.

**14. Company is up for sale or bought out**

If you suddenly notice that your company goes up for sale or is bought out by another company, you need to get ready for something big. Normally, jobs will be lost. But you may wish to consider hanging on to see what will happen to your position. As least if you are terminated you should normally expect that you will receive a monetary severance package. But, don't hold your breath. Companies do not always do what they should, do they? This may be an excellent time to transition into a new career you have always wanted to try.

I have a section devoted to starting your own business or new career in my first book: *Show Your Money Who's Boss. You CAN Regain Control over Your Finances.*

## 15.   Company profits drop significantly

The vast majority of the companies in America are now in this boat together. Watch this one in conjunction with other signs. Taken alone, this one does not necessarily mean that the end is near. But it may mean that. Use your best judgment here.

## 16.   You are offered a pay decrease

Your best response to this offer may be to smile and accept it. Smiling and accepting a pay decrease may buy you the time you need to find other work while still receiving a paycheck. But to be very realistic, as soon as you leave the presence of the supervisor who gave you the axe, begin submitting your résumé as quickly as possible. Try to get off the sinking ship before you go down with it. The only logical reason to consider staying on is if you are nearing retirement and do not wish to undergo the rigors of a job search at this time in your life. Who knows, you may be able to ride out the recession.

## 17.   Your responsibilities change to meaningless fluff or your workload is reassigned or reduced

This is a dead giveaway that you are soon to be toast. Get on your home phone or home computer and begin checking for other jobs. Burn some shoe leather. Get your résumé out as quickly as possible, set up as many interviews as you possibly can, and seek a new job. Like the ancient Babylonian King Belshazzar, you have just seen the handwriting on the wall as recorded in Daniel Chapter 5 in the Bible. Read what was written and get out.

## 18.   You notice an unusual number of high-level meetings between managers

Under normal business conditions, managers are constantly having meetings. Should you detect an abnormal number of meetings, you are probably right to assume that something unusual is in the air. Ask for hints as to what is going down. See whether you observe other signs that something is happening around the workplace.

**19.  Company begins outsourcing jobs overseas**

So many American companies have gone down this one-way street. In reality, it is the street of no return. Once outsourcing begins, it is only a matter of time until layoffs begin or people are reassigned to other jobs or other locations. Sometimes outsourcing spells closure for the office, agency, firm, corporation, plant, or factory where you work. Outsourcing is a major warning sign that things are about to change. Since the decision to either lay employees off or close the company has already been made, it will usually be nothing more than a matter of time until mass layoffs will take place.

**20.  Managers begin talking up the "New Direction" the company is about to take**

This is usually a sign that a takeover or sellout is coming or that someone is in the process of buying, reorganizing, or selling, your company. "New Directions," often require a reduction in numbers of the available workforce. If company A merges with company B, and the two are melded together, there will often be a need to trim back on the workforce to eliminate duplications of departments or personnel. Flexibility is the key here. You may be reassigned and your responsibilities may change. It happens every day in America, and with the current economic situation, prepare yourself to see more of this in the future.

**21.  Bosses begin treating you and other employees differently, either cold or aloof**

There is no guarantee, but this is usually a dead giveaway that someone has been targeted for something, and it isn't going to be pretty. Be careful and shun temptations to go paranoid; the simple explanation is that your boss may just be having a bad week. Many bosses seem to be cold and aloof much of the time. It makes one wonder how people who lack people skills get to be bosses or supervisors in the first place, doesn't it? If the behavior doesn't change and you still get the "cold shoulder," you may be up for being laid off or terminated, and the boss is giving you tons of non-verbal hints without even knowing that he is giving them. You may wish to start looking for a new job immediately.

## 22.   Company makes the news

Of course, it depends upon what type of news they are making. You only have to be concerned with bad economic news. If you work for a national or international company and you hear that they anticipate 5,000 layoffs within 30 days, you need to be concerned. Start looking for another job, but consider continuing to work where you are for a little longer. It may be that you will be unaffected and continue to maintain your status as an employee. The 5,000 jobs may all be from the closing of the plant three states away.

## 23.   Company goes high-tech and machines begin doing the work of people

This is another sure-fire sign that people are about to be replaced in the near future. It is possible that you will be one of the ones who remain to service the machines, but unless you have been trained to do this type of work, pack your bags and be ready to find another job.

## 24.   You are asked to train a new employee how to do your job

Some bosses must think that some of their employees are totally brain-dead if they think the employee doesn't know what is happening when they are asked to train someone else to do their specific job. This happens thousands upon thousands of times per year, and it usually means that you are about to be replaced by the younger, lower paid person that you are training. "Does it mean that I am about to be terminated?" No, it is not a guarantee that you will lose your job. However, the odds are certainly not in your favor.

### 25.  Company has difficulty making payroll

When the boss comes around and hints that you may not be paid on payday, you can figure that your company is on the skids and that it is facing a work shut-down. This is not an indictment against you but an indictment against the company, its managers, or the economy. Hold out for as long as you wish, but you had better consider finding another job as soon as possible. They are having cash-flow problems, and that usually means that their cash will stop flowing into your pocket.

If your company issues paychecks to everyone a few days ahead of a regularly scheduled payday, it is usually a sign of a definite and an immediate mass layoff. If this happens, your layoff is certain and is only a day or two away. The sad thing is that this can come with no prior warning. Tragically, some employees have felt secure about their jobs on Wednesday, only to discover that they were unemployed by Friday.

### 26.  Managers begin saying that things are no longer going to be the same

This is akin to number 20, but it can be distinguished from it in that he may be talking about a mass layoff, not a buyout by another company. A mass layoff involves 50 or more people, and there have been several thousands of them in America over the past several months of 2008-2009. What should the average person do if their boss said something like that to them? They should start looking for another job immediately. The boss was trying to drop a hint and attempting to give the person a head-start on getting another job. Be sure and thank him for the head's-up.

### 27.  Managers begin taking other jobs

They are like rats jumping off a sinking ship. If you notice this phenomenon taking place, it sure seems that you should begin looking for another job with a sense of extreme urgency.

## 28.   Owner or managers begin losing interest in the company

It may be a slight nuance, but this differs from the statement above because there is no sense of urgency on the owner's or managers' part to find other employment. It could mean that the job is scheduled to last another year or it could mean that the company is up for sale and that information will not be made public until a buyer is found. Ask your boss for information. If you can't get any information from your boss, then listen carefully for any hints that may slip. This could buy you more time to find another job.

## 29.   Corporate executives you have never seen before begin visiting your company

Again, you are put into a position to have to read between the lines. They may be there for purely good reasons and have nothing to offer but good-will. On the other hand, they may be bringing ultimatums, which if not met may spell doom for the company you work for. About all you can do is to listen for hints and be prepared to have to find another job.

## 30.   Others signs you can spot coming

No two companies, businesses, plants, universities, banks, factories, law or investment firms, or accounting firms, are exactly alike. Many of the 29 warning signs above would apply to most individual situations, but you are in a position to be able to tell what is going on in your company far more than I. Make your own observations and conduct your own listening sessions. You may be surprised at just how much information you will be able to pick up by just paying more attention than the average person you work alongside.

### To Spare Yourself Needless Pain

1.   Resist the temptation to read into your company's situation things that are not really there.

2.   Do not quit your job based solely on your interpretation of these warning signs because you could be wrong.

Look for significant corroborating evidence before deciding anything.

3.  If a layoff or closure is coming, find a new job as quickly
    as possible. But, before you accept a new job, check
    out your new company's stability and carefully weigh
    the risks of leaving your current job.

4.  Quit your current job ONLY after you have a new job in
    hand.

Now let's turn our attention to proven strategies others
have used to rise to the top in their companies.

# Chapter 8
# Getting the Raise or Promotion You Deserve

There are many things you can do to position yourself for a well-deserved raise or promotion. Extra effort will be required on your part, but will be a natural result of the layoff proofing process you apply to yourself and your job. Policies concerning raises and promotions vary widely from company to company and from boss to boss. Use the following ideas as starting points and then add specific ideas of your own that fit your unique company. If you have made the commitment to layoff proof yourself and the commitment to follow it up by your actions, you will find that raises and promotions are definitely in your future. They are within your reach. They are awaiting the people who are willing to earn them. Like diamonds lying on top of the ground, they are waiting to be picked up, go get them.

Do you remember reading about the gingerbread cookies in chapter one? We talked about refusing to be just another cookie-cutter employee, and that one of the most decisive things you could do to layoff proof yourself was to break out of the cookie-cutter mold. At this point in the process you should be experiencing a new level of confidence about layoff proofing yourself. Many others have succeeded and so can you. If you are making progress and are ready to advance to a higher level, consider the next step, the stuff that raises, promotions, and job opportunities are made of.

## Start by Smashing The Cookie-Cutter Mold

The next decisive step involves making a decision that could have major ramifications in many areas of your life including: your career, your confidence and comfort levels, raises and promotions, job opportunities, and others. Reaching the next level is a multifaceted process. 1. Realize that breaking out of the cookie-cutter mold is not enough. 2. Decide to smash the cookie-cutter mold instead. 3. Systematically implement the changes you choose to make. 4. Evaluate your progress and make any needed modifications. 5. Translate your layoff proofing experiences into action. 6. Work to earn a raise, promotion, or job opportunity. 7. Add any others you feel are necessary.

You will find that boldly taking the next step and smashing the mold has a bittersweet benefit...it will be impossible for you to ease back into the comfort zone of the cookie-cutter life. When your mold is broken you will not be able to sink back into the same rut you were in; in fact, you will not want to go back. This means that you can never be the same employee, supervisor, or boss, you once were. Breaking the mold is a powerful and positive means of expressing your dissatisfaction, defiance, and your commitment to make permanent changes that will distinguish you from the vast majority of the employees, supervisors, or bosses where you work. This act of defiance will distinguish you, or set you apart as someone who is ready to advance far beyond where you are today.

## Layoff Proofing Should Be Fun

Though it may be very challenging at times, layoff proofing yourself, smashing the cookie-cutter mold, and getting the raise or promotion you deserve should be processes from which you derive great satisfaction. It should be fun. Consider the following possibilities.

- Approach it with enthusiasm
- See it as something to enjoy and bring personal satisfaction

- Derive a deep sense of inner joy…you are doing something highly significant and worthwhile
- Enjoy great fulfillment in how it benefits you, your family, and your future
- Make a game of it. You may choose to enter it as competition with yourself, your job, your spouse, or a friend. Consider setting up a system of rewards… a special dinner, a shopping spree, a trip to the movies, or a special vacation
- Add your own ideas

You can choose to make it a positive experience that you and others around you enjoy, or you can allow the experience to turn you into a fire-breathing monster that others dread having to deal with.

**Fun Or Fire-Breathing Monster?**

A question comes to mind: "Will layoff proofing myself be fun or will it stress me out so much that it turns me into a fire-breathing monster?" Fortunately, you are the person who gets to answer that question. To help you decide which option you prefer, pretend that you decide to go all-out in your quest to layoff proof yourself. You design and implement the following plan…

For starters, you begin by changing the way you think, act, work, relate, respond, and react. Next, you change your attitude, work habits, behavior, outlook, work-ethic, and job performance. You then change the way you assume responsibility, complete projects, and perform your job. Next, you begin concentrating on the way you lead, supervise, and treat other people, including your family. You decide that all of these changes must be observable on a daily basis, so you create a mind game that you call: "Layoff Boot Camp." You play it in your mind every day on your way to and from work. You swell with pride when you realize that it is a little like Marine boot camp that your brother went through at Paris Island. Your new level of commitment will not allow you be the type of person who would just stick their toe into the water, experience the cold, withdraw it, dry it off, and then go back to the confines of the warm barracks and take a nap. Instead, you see the need to suit up mentally in full combat gear, lace up your boots, shoulder your pack, strap on your helmet, grab your rifle, grip your KA-BAR knife between your teeth, and jump into the water while breathing out fire and screaming: "Ooh-rah."

You are proud of yourself for elevating layoff proofing to a new level. You are engaging in life-changing, career-building, person-changing, company-changing, employee-changing, and boss-changing actions. You are living-out some seriously radical stuff. You decide that if you are willing to shatter the mold and become a radically different employee, you will succeed at almost anything you attempt. You come to the conclusion that most people can succeed at almost anything they set their minds to. The problem is that they never set their minds to do the things that would stretch them to their limits. You decide that people just aren't willing to pay the price for success. You are willing and you paid the price. Like Pheidippides, the legendary runner who ran from Marathon to Athens, delivered the message to the assembly that the Greeks had defeated the Persians, and then fell dead from exhaustion, you layoff proofed yourself to death.

**Balance Is The Key**

Except for two things, everything in that imaginary scenario was great. Those two things can be described in just four words: Too Much Too Fast. Question: can a person quickly accomplish all the things listed above and not be a total monster to work with or work for? Impossible. Expecting that kind of performance is far too ambitious for anyone to be expected to accomplish in short order. It would take years to incorporate all of those qualities into one's life and career. The story was written to illustrate the ridiculousness of trying to do too much too fast. It was hype.

The point is that you have to decide how far you will go with the layoff proofing model. Accept the challenge to neither be too easy nor too tough on yourself. Too many people have been so easy on themselves that they have grown lazy. Others have been so tough on themselves that their lives, the lives of those working alongside them, and the lives of their families are now characterized by pure misery. Don't do that to yourself, to anyone you love, or to anyone you work with. It is not worth it. Discipline yourself to push the envelope toward its limits, but know when and where to stop.

Decide on the changes you feel that you need to make and would like to make and then and only then make them. A good rule of thumb would be to push yourself far beyond what you normally would do, while doing only the things that would benefit you, your family, your fellow employees, and the company where you work. Allow your notable work experiences along with learning to layoff proof yourself to become turning points in the way you perform your job.

Muster the courage to climb to the next level. It is really not as difficult as you may think. Remember, as unfortunate as it is, more than half of the employees where you work aren't interested in making any personal improvements. Therefore, any substantive efforts you make to improve yourself and your company will be noticed, welcomed, and rewarded.

**Layoff Proofing Secrets Revealed**

"OK, how do I smash my cookie-cutter mold?" The answer lies in the profound but often overlooked hidden secret about layoff proofing yourself and your job: layoff proofing is an attribute of both your heart and your mind. Genuine layoff proofing and getting the raise or promotion you deserve is far more than just cleaning up your desk, working a little harder, and putting on a good face when the boss comes around. Layoff proofing is all about change. It is change from the inside out, not change from the outside in. Once the process begins in your heart and mind, it can then be translated into actions through your attitude, behavior, habits, deeds, performance, and into other significant areas of your life. That is why true layoff proofing can remain viable for an indefinite period of time. It is lasting and effective because it springs from deep within a person. True layoff proofing is internal, not external.

## Assessment: To Evaluate your Progress, Consider the Following Questions

1.  Have you determined to break out of and smash your cookie-cutter mold?
2.  Are you willing to refuse to be like the other employees where you work?
3.  Are you committed to distinguishing yourself as someone the boss, supervisor, owner, or CEO can't do without?
4.  Are you ready to layoff proof yourself and your job?
5.  Are you determined to implement the necessary changes you decided you need to make?
6.  Are you committed to moving forward and refusing to look back?
7.  Are you committed to becoming one of the top employees in your company?
8.  Are you ready to get a raise, be offered a promotion, or find a better job?

If you can truthfully answer yes to all of those questions, you are ready to smash your cookie-cutter mold. "How do I smash the mold?" you ask. We will get to that in a moment, but first consider the following.

Most of the people who work alongside you are satisfied with the status quo. To smash the mold you have to dare to be different. You begin by distinguishing yourself from your coworkers. You have the potential to rise above their level as you begin applying principles from your past and present experiences, and add any new ones you have just learned.

There are many things you can do that will enable you to become one of the top employees in your company. Since your company and your job have distinguishing characteristics all their own, you will have to decide on your own game plan. Design a plan that fits your individual situation. Step back and take a week or a couple of weekends to analyze your job, your company, and your career goals. Next, develop your personal plan. Write it down. Refine it, revise it, sharpen it, and write it down again. Distill your plan into 5-10 principles or action items you wish to implement, and begin systematically applying them to your life and work situation. Now you will be able to approach your work with a plan in your heart and mind that will enable you transform yourself into the employee you want to become.

**First, Start On The Inside**

Before any attempt at layoff proofing yourself can be expected to achieve lasting results, it must spring forth from within your heart and mind. This is not some sort of transcendental gobbelty-gook, it is just a common sense way of saying that the desire to succeed must come from within yourself. You can't layoff proof yourself to please your boss, your spouse, your parents, or anyone else. If you want to layoff proof yourself you will do it because you want to do it. Unless you want to layoff proof yourself it will never happen. It is that simple.

Once you have decided that you want to layoff proof yourself, everything will take on a different meaning. Have you ever known someone to have a prepaid college education and then flunk out? It is obvious that they didn't want to be there. Have you ever known a person that was set up in business by their parents only to see the business fail? Again, it is obvious that their heart was not in it. Once you decide to layoff proof yourself, nothing will be able to hold you back.

## Practices that Lead to Raises and Promotions

The following principles may be translated into actions in your life. Implementing these actions will position you for that well-deserved raise, promotion, or job offer. Depending on the company where you work, you may see immediate results; others may have to wait as their potential raise or promotion goes through the pipeline or the appropriate channels your company has in place.

## Work Smarter, Work Harder, and Produce Meaningful Results

This first principle is so simple that it shouldn't have to be stated. However, since many have missed discovering it somewhere along the way here it is: One of the best strategies you can implement to earn a raise or promotion is to work hard. We have all heard the mantra: "work smarter, not harder." People have rallied around that phrase as though it were some magical formula for success. It may come as a surprise to some to know that there is no law that says you can't do both. A key part of the true formula for success is this: "work smarter AND work harder." Business owners, bosses, and supervisors respect and appreciate hard work. If you build a reputation of being someone who works hard, you will have won the biggest part of the battle against layoffs. If your decisions, actions, and work-ethic impress your boss that you not only work hard but that you also work smart, you will be seen as one of his most valuable assets.

However, working hard and working smart for the sake of hard and smart work is not enough. For them to pay off, they must offer meaningful results, be valuable to the company, and produce the results your job demands. If you don't produce the results your boss, supervisor, or company expects, then all of your work is relatively meaningless. Most business owners, bosses, and supervisors are results-oriented. Choose to focus your energies on the things you can do to make a difference for your boss, your company, and yourself. In light of these statements, my new formula for success is: **"Work smarter and work harder and produce meaningful results."** Refuse to waste precious time and energy on things that provide no results. If you are achieving notable results for the department or the company, you are home-free.

A smart employee will learn what his or her boss expects. Once he or she knows what is expected, they develop a plan to accomplish those expectations. If you don't know what you are supposed to be doing on your job, your first priority should be to discover what your boss expects. Once you have a clear understanding of those expectations, you need to produce those results. Determine to be one of the very best employees your company has at meeting those expectations and you should excel. A raise, promotion, or job opportunity is in your future.

**Distinguish Yourself From Others**

Don't settle for being satisfied to be just like everyone else. If you go to a new car dealership and walk through row after row of new cars, you will find that most of them are exactly the same. If you are one of 100 cookie-cutter employees, you need to do things that will distinguish you from the other 99. The very best way to distinguish yourself is by having an above average work-ethic and level of performance or output.

A superior work-ethic would include most, if not all of the following:

- works hard and achieves all expectations
- works smart and has a sense of urgency about job
- produces meaningful results
- possesses high standards of excellence
- is seldom late for work and stays until the appointed time to leave
- minimizes all complaining and griping
- is cooperative, pleasant, and easy to get along with

- is dependable and attempts to excel at work
- produces for company, department, or superior
- is efficient, timely, prompt, and punctual
- has an ability to set and achieve goals
- pulls share of load and more
- does the opposite of the 33 things that result in lay offs

It is safe to say that if you are achieving most of the attributes from this list and are doing a good job in the performance or output departments as well, you are doing all you can do to position yourself for a raise or promotion. Of every 100 employees, at least 75-80 would look at the list above and say, "No way, that's ridiculous." This is where you can begin to distinguish yourself from all the others and move yourself high up the boss' list of employees that are "keepers."

If you want more money or a promotion, then go get it. The highest paid people know how to make goals and achieve them. They have learned how to exceed what is expected of them. How hard would it be to move yourself up to join the ranks among the top echelon of employees where you work? Depending upon your specific job situation, that may be very easy or very difficult. What if you set a goal to move yourself into the top 10% of the employees in your company and worked extra hard to achieve that goal? The result is that you would begin to distinguish yourself as an achiever or a producer. You would expect to see your status rise rather quickly. Your boss would begin to respect you more than ever and you would be seen as a valuable part of the team where you work. This may be easier to pull off than you might think. We will examine that next, but first, look at the numbers for a moment. To place yourself within the top 10% means this: if there are 2,500 people who work where you work, you would move yourself up to the top 250. If 500 people work there, you would advance to the top 50, or, if 100 work there, to the top 10.

You say: "That sounds good, but how would I go about doing that?"

Consider using the following worksheet:

**My Plan to Rise to the Top 10% Where I Work**

**My Goals: Actions I will take to layoff proof myself:**

**My Strategies: Changes I am willing to implement to get there:**

**Action Plans:**
**Three things I can begin doing today:**

1.

2.

3.

**Five things I can do this week: (Then five more for the next week.)**

1.

2.

3.

4.

5.

**One result I would like to achieve one month from today:**

**Three results I would like to achieve three months from today:**

(Personalize this worksheet to fit both yourself and your job situation.)

Use this worksheet, or one of your own, to develop a personalized plan that will propel you upward in your career. Invest a significant amount of time and thought into it. Once you have identified the things you will implement, go for it. Dedicate yourself to working your plan. Don't be afraid to make any necessary adjustments to your plan as you go along. "What if I fail?" you ask. One thing is certain; you will fail if you do not try. So what if you fail to become one of the top 10% of employees at your company? You may only be able to elevate yourself into the top 20%. Great job, you have just succeeded in doing all you can do to layoff proof yourself while positioning yourself for a well-deserved raise or promotion. You are far better off than all of those who did nothing at all. Plus, you will have learned some new skills and improved your job performance while laying the groundwork for future raises or promotions. Your time wasn't wasted; on the contrary, it was time very well spent.

**Monitor Your Progress...Self Evaluation**

- Use a worksheet to state your goals, and as a checklist to monitor your progress
- Compare your current job performance with your performance of a month ago
- Ask a trusted friend at work to give an honest appraisal of your progress
- Compare the numbers: this month's sales statistics, new accounts, and other tangible figures with last months' numbers

- Don't be afraid to make any necessary adjustments to your plan as they are needed
- Devise other personalized ways to monitor your progress.

## Move Up Incrementally

Just a brief word of caution; there is reason for concern when implementing this strategy. There will be some large temptations ahead of you, including the temptation to: 1. Bite off more than you can chew. 2. Expect results overnight. 3. Become discouraged. 4. Give up.

If entered into too aggressively, the expected results could be your production falling, your morale suffering, a building resentment toward yourself and your company, followed by giving up on the process entirely. Be as aggressive as you want, but don't expect to be the number one employee in three-weeks. Give yourself a lot longer than that. Your rise to the top will not happen overnight. It may take several months or longer. But, it can be done and it will be something you will look back upon, congratulate yourself, and pat yourself on the back. Be patient. During some weeks or months you will make a lot of progress, while others will see less. This is perfectly normal...be patient with yourself.

Take an incremental approach as you develop your own personal strategy to move yourself up to become one of the top 10% of employees. It will help to set your goal to break into the top 50% or so at first. As you achieve that goal, set your sights on the top 30% and so on. As you are moving up the ladder of success, your movement will be noticed. Once you have achieved your ultimate goal, moving yourself into the top 25% or top 10%, you will be attracting the attention that will result in getting you noticed very quickly. Develop your strategy and set goals for yourself to achieve. Don't be satisfied to be just one of 100, 500, or 1,000 cookie-cutter employees. When raises and promotions are awarded, most employers reward their top performers. Your objective is to become one of the top performers where you work. Likewise, if layoffs begin in your company, they will likely start at the bottom of the list. If you are in the top 25% you should remain untouched unless either the company or your department has to shut down completely.

At some point along your personal journey of adding value to your position and advancing yourself, you may wish to consider scheduling an appointment with your supervisor or boss to discuss a few things. "What, a raise or a promotion?" you ask. Not on your life. You would want to save that for a later discussion, (we will discuss timing in a moment.) It would need to take place only after you have made significant strides forward in your output or production. What you need to discuss with them now is the fact that you wish to contribute more to help your business or company succeed during these tough economic times. You could tell them that you want to beef-up your job performance and become an achiever. After your boss picks himself up off the floor from the shock he experiences from having an employee say something so radical, you can ask him to suggest things you can begin doing to make yourself a more productive employee. If you are up for it, you may even wish to ask him if there are any new tasks or responsibilities you can perform that will help the company.

By now, 99% of bosses will be wondering what has come over you. They may be thinking that you must have just sustained a bump to your head or they may even question your sanity. If you do decide to schedule such an appointment, first be sure and develop a game plan. Make sure that it is well thought out and very specific in purpose. Then, stay on task and do not deviate from what you wish to communicate.

Be ready for your boss to ask you this question: "Why do you suddenly want to do these new and unusual things?" You may choose to tell them that you are attempting to layoff proof yourself and your job or you may choose not tell them that. It is entirely up to you. If you want, you can blame it on this book. Whatever approach you decide to take, you will need to have an honest answer. As you leave your appointment, you want to leave your boss thinking: "Wow, I wish all my employees were as motivated as that." You don't want to leave with them thinking: "Wow, I think she or he is crazy."

"Do I really have to schedule this appointment?" No, not unless you want to. Use your better judgment here. With some supervisors or bosses and in some job settings you may actually harm yourself by scheduling such an appointment. The last thing you want to happen now is for your boss to think that you are up to something, are attempting to manipulate him, that you have lost your mind, or that you are only wanting to get in good with him.

Your best plan of attack may be to allow your actions, deeds, and performance to do your speaking for you.

**Volunteer For the Tough Assignments**

One quick way to be noticed is to volunteer for the tough assignments.

Caution: don't rush to volunteer for something unless you are reasonably certain that you have the skills to pull it off successfully. Should you volunteer for something extremely difficult and fail to achieve the expected results, the experience may have a negative affect upon your supervisor's opinion of you. That is another one of the last few things you want to happen. Be brave, but be careful. Take risks, but be resourceful. Be aggressive, but be circumspect. Think this one through before you get in over your head.

If you pull it off and are able to achieve success when taking on an extremely tough assignment, you will be labeled as successful. The owner, boss, or supervisor will definitely notice. You may even be deemed somewhat of a hero...depending upon the severity of the assignment in which you succeeded. If you win at your first tough one, you will be assigned another. If you win at a second, they will give you a third. By the third win, you will be seen as indispensable to the company and should be able to retain your job indefinitely. With a few successes under your belt, you will become a likely candidate for a raise or a promotion. After you have had several successes you will find that you are in a position to ask for a raise or promotion. When you are ready to ask, make a list of your accomplishments, develop your strategy, schedule an appointment with the appropriate person, and go into the meeting and make the strongest case possible for yourself and the raise or promotion you deserve. Be aware that you may have to negotiate, so brush up on your negotiating skills.

However, there may be an obvious negative result to your success. You could be fired because you may be seen as a threat to your boss, supervisor, manager, or even the owner. This kind of behavior would be nothing more than pure envy or jealousy, but it has cost some people their jobs. Be cautious for this very reason; if you begin showing other people up, you may be the one they decide to lay off because you are making others look bad. Don't be threatened, and refuse to allow this potential threat to hold you back in any way. However, give a lot of thought to how you would handle the negative reactions other people may have toward your successes.

**Become a True Team Player**

Admittedly, this is a cliché. However, the concept of team has great value. Many of today's professional teams are built around superstars. This practice rarely works in the average workplace. Unless you are self-employed, being a team player is far superior to being a solo performer. If you do work for yourself, you can be or do anything you choose.

When you work for someone else, one of the best things you can do for yourself is to transform yourself into a team player with a purpose. Your purpose is to bring success to your job and your company. Your success will bring revenue or profit to the company and ultimately to you as well.

Consider the value of being a team player. The fastest running back on the best NFL team would look like a junior high school running back and be deemed a total failure without his offensive line blocking for him. Unfortunately, the running backs receive most of the glory along with the fat paychecks. But it is the guys in the trenches and downfield blockers that are the ones that make his spectacular runs and touchdowns possible.

The same is true of the great NFL quarterbacks. They would be worthless as quarterbacks without their offensive lines. They wouldn't be able to pass, hand off the ball, or run it themselves without the other 10 men on their teams.

This concept is further illustrated by the strands of a rope. If you were to unravel one strand from a rope you would find that it is easily broken by your bare hands. When you place five strands together and try to break them you will meet with more resistance. Group 10 strands together and it now becomes difficult to break them. Group 20 strands together and you can hardly break them at all. Group 200 together and they can support the weight of a large-sized automobile.

When a group of people work together for a common result, they can do astounding things. Demonstrate to the boss the fact that you can get along with other people and can work with them. Business owners, bosses, and supervisors love team players. They expect cooperation from you as one of their employees. Don't be someone who disappoints them.

Since jealousy is quite common in many work places, team players are looked upon very positively by management. Do everything within your power to foster a sense of camaraderie instead of jealousy. Being a team member is not something you announce, it is something you demonstrate. You model the fact that you are a part of the team by the way you work with other people. Your respect, co-operation, sharing in successes and failures, appreciation of others, acknowledgement of another's skills and abilities, all contribute to your team membership. If you go to work tomorrow and suddenly announce to your co-workers that you are now on the team they may look at you as though you are crazy. Just be a team member, don't announce it; allow your actions to speak louder than any words you might utter.

Now, consider this concept. This is where your strategy to move yourself up into the top 10% can be applied. Every football team has men who stand on the sidelines or sit on the benches. Why do those men stand along the sidelines? It's because the best players are on the field playing the game. The men standing on the sidelines and sitting on the benches are important. They are reserves. The best players are the starters. You need to set your sights on becoming a "starter" at your place of employment.

Is it permissible for individual team members to excel? Yes, great individuals who excel cause the team to excel. Never be afraid or ashamed to do your very best. The best will be rewarded while the average goes unnoticed. The Bureau of Labor Statistics suggests that people actually work approximately four hours per day. Think what you could do by working just two more hours per day than the average person. Resist the temptation to work two more hours on some aspect of your job that will go unnoticed. Look for something that will be noticed and will make a difference then do it. Only you can decide what to do to get yourself noticed by your supervisor or boss. Put your thinking-cap on, come up with a plan, and implement it today.

**Win the Attitude Battle**

How would you respond if your teen came and asked you, "Hey mom, or dad: Who is in charge of your work attitude? It's your supervisor, right?" What would you say: "That's a stupid question with a stupid answer?"

No, you would say something like: "Where did that question come from?" Then you would follow that question by saying something like: "I am in charge of my own attitude, just like you are in charge of yours." The point is that each one of us is totally responsible for our own attitudes. Though we often try, we can't really shift that responsibility upon someone else.

Being in charge of one's attitude is like being in charge of one's car. The person who is behind the steering wheel is the person in charge of driving the car. Let's pretend that your friend's car is broken and since you both work for the same employer you give them a ride to work. As you are driving they suddenly say: "You just missed our turn." You look over at them and say: "I don't know what you are talking about." Your friend says: "I'm sorry, that's the street I take every morning and I assumed you followed the same route." You respond: "No, I didn't know about that street. This is the way I have driven to work every morning for the past 10 years." If you are the driver, you are in charge of your car. You drive it on the route you choose to follow. Passengers or even the radio traffic reporter may suggest that you should take a different route, but ultimately, you are in charge of your car and where it takes you. If you don't believe me, try telling the next police officer who pulls you over for going a little too fast that the guy in the passenger seat is the culprit because he is the one who told you to go fast.

What can I do to transform my lousy "I hate my job, or I hate my boss," attitudes? Let's be honest, some jobs are totally undesirable. You may have one of those jobs. What you need is an immediate job change or boss change, but good jobs and good bosses are getting tougher to find these days. Every job has certain aspects that are undesirable. The key to transforming a lousy work attitude is to pick out one or more positive aspects of your job that you like and concentrate on them instead of the 95 other reasons you despise your job or your boss. Refuse to allow your job, your boss, your coworkers, your friends, or your family to de-termine the attitude you will have toward your job and your career. Muster the courage to dare to be different.

Take charge of your own attitude. Choose to focus and direct your attitude and energies in the directions you determine are best for you. Just as you are in control of your car when you are driving to work every day, you are to be in control of your attitude. Do not give someone else the power over your attitude and outlook. You, and not some other person, should determine the attitude you have. Can't others influence my attitude? Yes they can. Anyone and everyone you allow to influence it will do so. Admit-tedly, your attitude can be impacted by many internal and external forces. One of your most important jobs is being the gatekeeper for your own attitude. You have the option to choose the circumstances, events, factors, and people that you will allow to influence your attitude. You also have the option of choosing to prohibit them from influencing your attitude as well. In short, it is your attitude, so you need to be in charge of it.

**Boost Your Morale**

Morale is an intangible and illusive quality that every-one loves to talk about but rarely does anything about. Two reasons for this is that morale can be hard to define and even more difficult to comprehend. Morale is attitude in action. If you have a workplace that is permeated with people who have bad attitudes, collective morale will be terrible. If the workplace is teeming with people who have positive attitudes, morale will be high. One of the greatest mistakes many people make concerning morale is assum-ing that someone or something can magically boost their morale for them.

If you are waiting for a highly motivated supervisor or a large pay increase to boost your morale, you are wast-ing your time. Refuse to wait for someone to appear out of nowhere and be your personal morale booster. I hate to be the bearer of bad news, but if your morale is going to be improved, you will have to take the necessary steps to improve it for yourself. Your morale is your attitude in action. If you want your morale to be elevated, it will come as a result of the elevation of your attitude. Don't sit around and wait for your boss, your supervisor, or a raise to boost either your attitude or morale. Waiting on some external factor like that may take years. To see a boost in your morale, change your attitude.

One of the best ways you can change your attitude about your job is to select one or more positive things about your job and concentrate your efforts on them. No, the undesirable aspects of your job will not go away. However, your perspective can be changed. You can deliberately choose to concentrate your thoughts, efforts, and energies upon more of the positive than negative things. While it is possible that you will experience a shift in your morale overnight, it probably will take a little longer than that for most people. Give yourself some time and it will happen. The Bible issues a challenge when it asks believers to be "transformed by the renewing of your mind" Romans 12:2 (NIV). Anyone can ask God to begin this process of transformation within them as they deal with their morale and attitude.

**Contribute to the Success of Your Company**

You were hired to work for your company for a reason. The person who made the decision to hire you believed that you could perform a specific job for their company. What was the reason they hired you as opposed to someone else? Perhaps it was because someone recognized a skill-set you possess. It may have been your track record at the place you previously worked. It could have been your educational credentials, or the potential someone spotted within you that would benefit the company. Perhaps it was your winning attitude or sense of confidence. People are hired for a multitude of reasons.

Now that I have a job what should I do? Do what you were hired to do. Do that and more. Give your job your best effort. Give it 100%. If you do this, you will rise above more than 90% of your fellow employees. When a new employee is hired and begins working, they go through several phases as they acclimate themselves into their new job. One of the final phases that people experience is finding their comfort level. It is a level of work that they settle into and feel comfortable doing. Unfortunately, many employees find their comfort levels, get stuck in them, and remain there for many years. That is why most employees only work about four hours out of an eight hour shift. If you are willing to stretch yourself beyond what you are comfortable with, learn new things and take on new responsibilities, you will go much farther than the average Joe who works alongside you. What could you do for your production level if you increased your work time from four hours to six hours per day? Your output would soar. Your work level would increase and theoretically you would make more money for your company. Why should I care whether I make more money for my company? When you are making more money for your company, you are also making more money for yourself. The more successful you are in your job, the more successful your company will become. The more successful your company becomes, the more potential you have for getting a raise and for layoff proofing your job.

For example, suppose you work in retail and you are now selling an average of $100 per hour. That translates into $800 per day for every day you work. If you work 23 days per month you are selling an average of $18,400 per month. That is a lot of money. Now, let's play the "what-if game." What would happen if you were able to double your sales and begin selling $200 per hour, $1,600 per day, and $36,800 per month? Do you think your boss would notice? Do you think he would be inclined to give you a raise if you went to him after four months of dramatically increased sales, showed him your stats, and asked for a raise? If you have doubled your monthly sales and maintained them for four consecutive months, a dramatic increase such as that almost guarantees that you are in a position to receive a handsome increase. However, some bosses are very myopic and stingy with money, so you may have to sell him or her on the idea. Other bosses would see your potential raise as a game to be played with you. They would like to see just how skilled you really are as a salesperson. Don't be afraid to sell your boss on the idea that you have doubled your sales and, therefore, you deserve a decent raise for doing so. Let him or her know that a good raise would be a great incentive for you to sell even more. Finally, some companies are structured so that they can only give increases when employees come up for annual reviews. If that is true where you work, you will have to wait until that time to be rewarded.

Now, you don't have to be in retail for this principle to apply. No matter what you do or where you work, if you can increase your productivity or work output level you should be able to receive some significant pay raises. Coupled with the raises should be a very significant sense of job security.

Doubling your output would be a challenge for anyone, and you may find that doubling your output is nearly impossible. However, if you are able to increase your output by 10% you will be ahead of 90% of the people you work with. Whether your job is making widgets, phoning customers, mailing billing statements, sales, or anything else, increasing your value to the company will bring its rewards. When it comes time to begin laying people off you will be the very last person to come to mind if you are listed in the handful of employees who are benefiting the company.

- **Invent creative solutions**

Many employees cause problems of one type or another. How would you like to make a major contribution to your company and also receive some above-average recognition at the same time? One of the quickest ways to achieve that recognition is to become a person who solves problems, instead of a person who creates them. If you can learn to solve problems and become the go-to guy or go-to-gal when it comes to problem solving, you will distinguish yourself above almost all of the other employees where you work. Begin by looking around your workplace for a problem you can solve. You may be tempted to develop a solution like: "Fire Bob or Tiffany." Now, it may be true that one or both of them should be fired, but unless you are the HR manager or owner, you may not have the authority to make that decision. The solutions you create should be solutions that will benefit your job and everyone who works there. I know of one specific situation where an employee was given a $5,000 cash award for devising a solution to a specific problem experienced by a major retail chain.

You can become a problem-solver. Identify a problem, solve it, and look for another to solve. Solve the second problem and look for a third problem to solve. Solve the third and look for yet another. You may develop your problem-solving skills by researching the topic and by practice. Develop this as one of your skills.

Should you be interested in developing or refining this skill to world-class proportions, you would be able write your own ticket for almost any job you want anywhere you want it.

- **Work with a sense of urgency**

Develop a sense of urgency about your work. Approximately 90% of the employees in your workplace do not have a sense of urgency about their jobs, themselves, their careers, or layoff proofing themselves. Should you choose to capitalize upon your fellow employees' shortcoming, you will strengthen your position tremendously. The people who take their jobs too casually don't really care whether they achieve anything much or not. If you want to distinguish yourself far above the average worker at your plant, business, or retail store; incorporate the following attitude into your work-ethic…"While I am at work, I will work as though my life depends upon it." The stunning truth is this: your work life may actually depend upon how urgently you go about performing your job. Always go the "extra mile."

• **Increase your survivability**

As much as you may not want to admit it, you probably don't know everything about your job or industry. Don't just waste your time at work. Be willing to learn from your job, from your supervisor, manager, or business owner, your customers, and your fellow employees. In many workplaces there are experts or masters in their fields; get to know some of them and learn from their treasure-trove of knowledge and experience. Pick out one or more of these experts and aggressively learn from them. Find out what makes them tick. Ask questions and observe how they do their jobs. Implement some of their strategies and work-ethics. You will better yourself and enrich your skills and abilities. Most companies offer training. Capitalize upon the learning opportunities that are available to you. Especially take advantage of any training offered by your company. Be sharper than the average employee, keep your antennae up at all times, and make yourself indispensable. Know what is going on around you, observe and ask questions, and take advantage of every opportunity to learn and improve yourself as a person and as an employee. Keep a journal or record of the things you are learning. Begin by writing down five things you have learned since becoming an employee on your current job. Become so motivated that you get excited about your job and actually go to work expecting to learn something new each day.

• **Practice the core values of honesty, integrity, and trust**

Your reputation is among the most valuable of your possessions. Are you known as an honest and fair employee? How about your integrity and trustworthiness? These attributes are among the greatest of workplace virtues. Stories abound of employee theft, dishonesty, and scandalous behavior. Dare to be different. Set your goals and sights higher than the average employee. Are you an employee that can be trusted with access to company secrets or proprietary information, money, Social Security numbers, personal information, account and credit card numbers? The path to gaining trust at work is simple: be trustworthy in all that you do. This begins by giving a full day's work for a full day's pay. That is followed on a daily basis by all your other actions.

**You are Layoff Proof and Ready for a Raise or Promotion**

Remember the ancient Chinese proverb: "A journey of 1,000 miles begins with a single step?" Since you started reading this book, you may have taken steps toward layoff proofing yourself and your job. You have learned how to smash the cookie-cutter mold, you have examined the secrets of layoff proofing yourself and your job, you have reviewed the practices that lead to raises and promotions, and you have been challenged to rise to the top 10% in the company where you work. Are you ready to make yourself layoff proof and begin working toward that well-deserved raise or promotion? You have the ball and the decision about what to do with it lies within you. Go for it!

"Now that I have accomplished a lot of positive things and have made giant strides forward, is it possible that I could still be laid off? You already know the answer to that question. In this unstable economy, anything can happen. Let's consider how to survive a layoff should you experience one.

# Chapter 9
# Learn From Life's Winners, Not Life's Whiners

There is something refreshingly poignant about that phrase. I have come to understand that winners always find ways to succeed, while whiners waste their lives complaining about being treated unfairly. The average company is burdened with an overabundance of whiners. In contrast, every company has its share of winners as well. Learning from life's winners should neither be confused nor compared to learning from life's whiners. However, both groups perform a great service for you and me. By example, winners teach us how to succeed. By default, whiners teach us how to waste our lives. The differences between learning from a winner and a whiner would be like comparing a high-performance Porsche with a Weed King riding lawnmower.

Some of the people where you work are highly motivated and have already successfully layoff proofed themselves and their jobs. Some are on the same career track as you and may be unreachable. Don't worry; you don't have to pass them all. Why make yourself miserable trying to get ahead of someone who has a track record of being highly successful and has an eight-year head start? Don't sweat it, you really don't have to be number one at everything you do.

If you work for a company that employs 200 people and you are among the top 20 employees, you have likely already achieved layoff proof status. If you feel that you are on the bubble and that there are people ahead of you in your quest to layoff proof yourself, then work hard and make your ascent closer to the top as you gain experience, tenure, and maturity. Apply the principles you have learned and set out to make yourself layoff proof.

One way to get on the fast-track to achieving success is to identify the top 10-20 people working at your company and learn their secrets of success. Talk to them, listen to them, observe them, and ask questions. Learn what works for them. Ask them to tell you why they are successful. They may communicate some valuable insights that would enable you to rise far above the average employee in your company. Learn this very important lesson; learn from life's WINNERS, not life's whiners.

Even winners experience defeats. Every single one of the greatest sports teams in history has endured many losses during their down seasons. Most of the greatest inventors of all time experienced more failures than successes. The most talented musicians, singers, and actors have encountered slumps. The greatest investors in history have picked many stocks that turned out to be duds. Great writers, including the likes of William Shakespeare, have had days when the words were just not there. No doubt, there were days when Leonardo da Vinci, Claude Monet, and Vincent van Gogh had difficulty painting at the levels they expected to perform. Even the greatest composers of all time, Johann Sebastian Bach, Ludwig van Beethoven, and George Frideric Handel experienced failures.

One thing many of the greatest people of history had in common was their determination to keep trying after experiencing failures. In addition to the wonderful world-changing contributions each one of them made, their abilities to keep going may be among the greatest contributions they ever made. The great people mentioned above knew the following principle instinctively: When you get knocked down you get back up, dust yourself off, and begin working toward your goal again. Learn from life's Winners, not life's whiners. Would you rather be compared to a Porsche or a Weed King?

A layoff, termination, or job loss does not label you as a loser. It labels you as someone who is human just like all the rest of us. An important thing about job failures is that they can serve as significant markers in our lives. These markers do not stand as sentinels marking our failures so much as they stand out as monuments marking our turning points. Turning points are moments when we make conscious decisions to make changes in our lives that will move us to new levels of achievement or in new directions entirely.

Join me in exploring the fact that there is life after layoff.

# Chapter 10
# There Is Life After Layoff

## Winners Rise Above Their Circumstances

Sometimes even winners lose their jobs. A common experience that links many highly successful people is that in their past they were fired from one or more jobs. People have a lot at stake when it comes to the possibility of losing their jobs. Layoffs are accompanied by a tremendous sense of loss. They can be as stressful as a death in one's immediate family. Suffering accompanies most layoffs. In addition to the employee who lost their job, those who suffer the most are one's spouse, children, and other dependents. They suffer because two of life's major dynamics have changed…a job, and income. Even though they are missing, life's needs continue. Along with the basic needs of food, clothing, and shelter, comes countless others as well. The difference is that while basic needs remain and monthly bills continue coming in, now the once stable income you enjoyed and depended upon is missing. Layoffs have a devastating impact upon everyone touched by them.

A layoff can be as stressful as experiencing a death in one's family. After the death of a family member, survivors work through their grief and ultimately come to the conclusion that they must continue living their lives. When someone is laid off they experience a plethora of emotions, including: anger, fear, rage, frustration, doubt, hate, bitterness, what-if thinking, and others. At some point during the grief process accompanying a layoff, the employee and their family decide that life must go on. They have to go on, their kids are still in school, their families still have needs, and the monthly bills continue coming in. No matter how much they would like to stop the merry-go-round and get off, they decide that they have no choice but to get back to living their lives once again.

No matter how bleak things appear or how difficult they become, there is life after layoff.

## Winners Refuse to Take it Personally

Unless you brought it on yourself, losing your job has nothing to do with you personally. In this tough economy, companies are forced to choose to take drastic steps for their own financial survival. Layoffs happen. With money tight and consumer spending down, some companies have had no choice but to begin laying off some of their workforce. They must do whatever it takes to survive.

Business owners aren't necessarily cruel people who enjoy seeing their employees suffer. However, if a company's survival means laying off 40% of their workforce they have no other option but to make that call. The fortunate ones are the 60% who remain employed. However, some companies are either so deeply in debt, or are unable to continue selling their goods or services that they will ultimately have to close their doors forever.

Unfortunately, the stark reality for some is that they find themselves unemployed, they have taken large financial hits, and they may not be able to find a job as quickly as they would like. Should you experience a layoff, consider the steps you can take which may help you survive financially and find another job. You may just be able to find a way to turn a devastating loss into a positive gain.

## Winners Develop Action Plans

If you find yourself impacted by a layoff, spring into action and develop a plan for survival and growth. Here are a few starting points for your consideration.

1. Talk to your HR department and sign up for unemployment.

2.  Contact all of your creditors and tell them what happened. Ask them to work with you by allowing you to make small minimum payments.

3.  Seek financial assistance from your church, family, friends, government programs, or private sources, Ask for a handout. Resist the urge to borrow money from a friend or family member, because you will most likely see the relationship change from friend to that of debtor. Keep your friendships viable. Don't ask to borrow money...you may never be able to pay it back.

4.  Begin seeking another job. Be honest with yourself and your family. It may take a while to find a job so apply to as many places as you possibly can.

5.  Trim back all spending.

6.  Eliminate all optional expenses you possibly can.

7.  Refuse to give up hope, make the mandatory adjustments and keep going.

8.  Use this time to better yourself and your family, not to embitter them.

9.  Don't beat yourself up. Know that things will get better someday. Thousands of other people have been in similar circumstances as you and survived. You can as well.

10. Don't give up. Research and discover ideas to earn money or launch a new career.

### Winners Provide Positive Leadership for Their Families

Your family is looking to you for positive leadership. In a negative financial situation they need the type of positive leadership you can provide. You will set the tone for how your family deals with the financial crisis you are experiencing. You will greatly influence your family's attitude, outlook, sense of hope, and faith. Be honest and realistic with yourself and your family. Things may get worse before they get better. Lead them to expect the best, but prepare for the worst. Remind them that there are millions of other

Americans who also need jobs and are struggling just like all of you.

One of the most important things you can lead your family to do is to come together and be supportive of one another. Layoffs often bring out feelings of bitterness, resentment, anger, rage, hopelessness, frustration, a sense of failure, and a dozen other negative things. More than ever before, your family needs to experience a sense of unity and a common purpose. They need to rally around one another for mutual support, and have goals to work toward. You can lead them to develop and achieve these goals.

Seek their ideas, input, and involvement in family decision-making processes. Make decisions together. This will create a sense of ownership of the goals you set as a family. Lead in setting financial goals geared to helping you survive the recession. This will be a great time for you to lead them through the process of prioritizing and making spending decisions. This spending plan is called a budget. Lead them in the area of financial discipline and cutting back all unnecessary spending. Provide the leadership to build a sense of unity and encourage your family to come together as you make the tough choices that lie ahead. Your choices may include things like housing, cutting back on optional spending, selling your second car, taking a second or part-time job to support the family, and a variety of other things that you face through the difficult days you are experiencing.

## Winners Understand that Extraordinary Times Require Extraordinary Responses

You have the opportunity to distinguish yourself from all the other job applicants in your area when entering your job search. One of the best ways you can distinguish yourself from others is to follow this principle: Extraordinary times require extraordinary responses. One of the extraordinary responses you may be forced to make is to take a job that is far less than what you are accustomed to...it is a matter of financial survival.

## Underemployment

Because of our extraordinary economic times you may have to work far beneath your abilities, levels of education, experience, skill, and training. Don't be surprised if you have to work at a job you consider to be far below what you deserve. I know a research chemist with a PhD that was laid off from a major university who now works as a cashier at a retail store. It is called survival. He hopes to one day return to his research job. But for now, he is happy to have a job. I know another man who worked his way up the ladder to become an assistant manager at a company that employs 125 people. Each night when he is scheduled to close the store, he personally cleans the restrooms. He does this in order to remind himself from where he came, and that he is better than no one else in the company. Needless to say, he has the respect of everyone who works there. Are you willing to humble yourself to that point? It's all about survival.

Most people would refuse to do a job like that. However, in times like these that may be the only type of job you can find. If that is the only job you can find, would anyone in their right mind blame you for taking it? That job might save your home, your family, and might just allow you to survive your financial crisis. Sure, there are much better jobs out there so go for them first, but don't be too good to take a lesser job if that's what it comes down to.

Businessmen are always saying that they just can't find anybody who wants to work. Everyone would like to have a high paying job with lots of prestige and great benefits. There are many jobs out there that are like that. But, if you sit back and refuse to work until you have one of those plumb jobs you may suddenly awaken ten years from now and find that you haven't worked for ten years. You have to start somewhere. You may have to consider taking a lower paying job to provide some income while looking for that better job you deserve. At least you will be bringing in some much needed income.

**Winners Identify their Options**

One of the most germane questions anyone can ask is: "What do I do if I am laid off or lose my job?"

**1. Identify all of your options.**

Take some time to reflect upon your situation. Write down every possible option that comes to mind. You may be surprised to find that you have more than you think.

**2. Weigh all your options.**

Examine every option from the list you just made. Discuss these options thoroughly with your family, a trusted friend, or others who will give you honest feedback. List the positives and negatives of every option.

**3. Decide what you want to do.**

Prioritize your list. See your layoff as the point of a new beginning in your life. Your layoff could be one of the best things that ever happened to you if it results in your doing something you always wanted to do but were unable to attempt.

**4. Develop a plan to achieve your goals.**

Settle upon a plan of action and begin working your plan. Your plan may be that of seeking new employment, retirement, or becoming an entrepreneur. Now that you have decided what it is that you want to do...do it.

**5. Renew your faith in yourself.**

Layoffs and job losses are devastating. The damage is inflicted on our emotions, self-confidence, self-worth, faith, and finances. Engage in thoughts, practices, and activities that will boost your morale and confidence. You are a valuable person. You are loved and needed.

**6. Place your ultimate faith in God.**

During times of uncertainty and crisis, people have benefited greatly from turning to the Lord for help. Turn to

Him, for He is the greatest resource that I and countless millions have ever had.

Up to this point I have outlined the most important principles related to layoff proofing. My goal was to challenge you to implement some of the common-sense principles that will help you layoff proof yourself and your job. I have saved the single most important principle for last.

**Winners Connect To The Ultimate Winner**

Real Winners connect to the ultimate winner and power source: Jesus. Let me explain as I share the foundational principle of my life. Like you, my wife and I have had our share of life's knocks, bumps, and bruises. We have had our share of successes and failures as well. We have experienced the personal struggles of unemployment, financial hardship, serious health issues, as well as traumatic experiences in the lives of our children. Of all that we have experienced, those involving our children were the toughest to deal with. Through our experiences we learned one of the greatest spiritual principles of all. We learned that while God neither removes nor insulates Christians from life's devastating problems, he is there to offer his awesome presence, his loving comfort, and his amazing grace. God is faithful.

Our son was moments away from death as a result of a SIDS incident when he was two months old. It was 3 AM and I was out of town on business when my wife heard him gasping for breath and rushed to his side. He had turned blue. She administered mouth-to-mouth and called 911. He spent three days in the hospital undergoing tests, wore a breathing monitor for the next six months, and experienced no further episodes. At age 17, he was one of four passengers in a car that crashed. Sadly, the accident claimed the life of the driver when they slammed into a power pole while travelling 70 miles per hour. By the grace of God, my son and the other young men survived. His seatbelt caused internal damages that required surgery and a week in the hospital. He later spent three tours of duty with his squadron in Iraq while serving his country. The Lord is good.

Recently, our daughter experienced a severe episode of HELLP Syndrome. She was in great physical condition and had experienced a normal pregnancy. She was in labor with her first child and had been admitted to the hospital. During labor, her liver ruptured. It ruptured with such force that a portion sheared off. Within moments, her doctors began infusing blood and performed emergency surgery in an attempt to save her life. This tragic event would have claimed her life had it not been for God's mercy and grace; the head trauma surgeon and team of doctors being on duty that particular weekend night; and the level-one trauma hospital where she was a patient. God intervened and spared her life. She was on life support and highly sedated over the next three days as her doctors performed two additional surgeries. When the crisis was over and it became apparent that she would survive, her doctors told us that they had infused a total of 24 units of blood to keep her alive. She spent the first 10 days of her 14 day hospital stay in ICU, and was blessed to be able to hold her daughter for the first time, two weeks after she was born. The Lord is good. We still have our daughter, a wonderful son-in-law, and a precious granddaughter as well.

Why do I mention these intensely personal events? To say that during the darkest hours of our lives we experienced God's presence in ways that words cannot describe. Jesus is the greatest source of faith, strength, power, peace, hope, and comfort. In addition, he is the greatest source of confidence, assurance, gentleness, understanding, acceptance, forgiveness, and love. The Lord is faithful. He was there for us when we needed him most. Though we had experienced his blessings before those events touched our lives, it was God's powerful presence and his amazing grace that provided the strength we needed to sustain us throughout those extremely trying times.

Again, one of the key spiritual principles we learned is that God neither removes, nor insulates Christians from ALL of life's difficulties, hardships, and devastating problems. Instead, he equips his children with the resources they need to face their problems and grow stronger as a result of having experienced them. God affirms the truths and principles they learned and were equipped with during times of difficulty and applies them to their present circumstances. God's resources are there to enable them to be victorious over the large and small issues of daily life. In addition, the daily blessings he gives his children are truly wonderful.

Looking back at the experiences I mentioned, plus a few others, I can honestly say that they all have had a positive impact within our lives. My wife and I experienced our greatest spiritual growth during and after those life-changing events. They taught us some of the greatest lessons, truths, and principles that we could have ever learned about the Lord and life itself. God is so good. Faith and a personal relationship with God are truly the most important foundations of life.

Anyone who has the desire can lead their family toward a wonderful spiritual relationship with the Lord. This does not mean that everyone will see the Lord the same way you do. It does mean that you can live your life in such a way that people will want to experience what you have, and when they ask you what you have that they are missing, you have the answer they need. When one reaches out to the Lord and discovers the joy of a relationship with him, he or she will discover the same sustaining power that my wife and I discovered. Jesus and Jesus alone can provide a lasting sense of purpose, direction, hope, friendship, and emotional support that are needed to get through this wonderfully complicated experience we call life.

We were created with a God-shaped void in our lives that no person or material thing can fill except God Himself. Unfortunately, many have tried to fill that void with everything except a relationship with God. Admittedly, many attempts are very satisfying. Many things can bring temporary relief from the emptiness, but the emptiness returns. While lying in bed late at night or early in the morning, some experience a deep feeling that something is missing, or is just not right. That haunting feeling of emptiness is best understood as one's soul craving for a relationship with God. Nothing less than a relationship with God can make that craving go away.

You can put yourself and your family in a position to receive God's blessings. The truth of the matter is that you will never know the extent of the wonderful blessings God will provide unless you put yourself in a position to receive them. God knows that you need encouragement and blessings. Two of your best sources for receiving daily blessings from the Lord are those of prayer and reading your Bible. A great starting point would be to spend a few moments each day in prayer, and then read a chapter from the Psalms or the Proverbs, and the Gospel of John. You will probably remember John 3:16 "For God so loved the world that he gave his one and only Son, that whosoever believes in him shall not perish but have eternal life."

How does one get to know Jesus personally? By FAITH.

- **F**orgiveness: repent, or turn away from your sins, and ask God to forgive all of them
- **A**ccept Jesus as your Lord and Savior
- **I**nvite him into every area of your life
- **T**ruth: discover God's life-changing truths in the Bible and begin following Jesus as Lord of your life
- **H**ave a great time worshipping God and growing in you relationship with him in a Christ-centered church

As I grew up, I embraced the teachings of Christ and the Christian faith as revealed in God's Word, the Bible. While an undergraduate student at a major university, I became actively involved in Campus Crusade for Christ International. When its founder, Dr. Bill Bright, visited our campus, he challenged several hundred students to be faithful in their daily relationship with the Lord. He emphasized that being a Christian and living one's Christian life must carry over into all areas of our lives. After college, I came to a greater understanding and appreciation of the wisdom of his statements. Upon graduation I moved to another state, completed graduate school, married, embarked on a career, and experienced life as a father.

I leave you with one of the positive truths that Bill Bright shared with us: "God loves you and offers a wonderful plan for the rest of your life." This is a truth you can count on. It is true no matter where you have been, no matter what you have done in your past, or no matter what you may be experiencing in the present. God really does love you, and wants to enable you to succeed. For me, true success comes through my relationship with Christ.

For more information about God's wonderful plan for the rest of your life and to discover how to know Jesus personally, check out Campus Crusade's website: **http://www. ccci.org/wij/index.aspx**

The Lord wants to bless you. He is on your side and wants to help in every area of your life. Draw closer to him, pray, and study the Bible every day. If you are not already involved in a church, do something good for yourself and seek out a Christ-centered church and begin building relationships with people there. The Lord and his people can offer friendship, acceptance, moral support, prayers, and many other blessings.

Today, I am enjoying life and the daily blessings of God as I grow in my relationship with the Lord and enjoy spending time with my wife and family. I enjoy working full-time, writing, and managing my web site. The foundational principle of my life continues to be my personal relationship with Jesus. Most, if not all of the concepts of this book are outgrowths of that relationship and my experiences as a Christian.

If you have been devastated with the loss of your job, your house, your family, or have sustained other tremendous losses, present those losses and yourself to the Lord. Invite him into your life and into your life's events, experiences, defeats, and victories. Ask him to equip you to handle the losses, to recover and grow through the process, and to enable you to grow stronger and closer to him because of them.

If you are already a believer, God wants to enable you to experience GROWTH.

- **G**row stronger in your relationship with God and other Christians. Spend time with God every day and engage in activities that will encourage your spiritual growth. Ask God to give you a passion for spiritual growth.

- **R**ecommit yourself to grow closer to God. Recession, layoffs, financial difficulties, and a poor economy can cause great stress. God can help you if you will draw closer to him. Get to know him intimately.

- **O**n Sunday, go to a Christ-centered church where you can serve God, make friends with other people, and make a difference with your life.

- **W**itness to others about your faith by telling them about Jesus. Don't just stand there, get involved. Ask God to use you to help other people.

- **T**ake charge of your personal spiritual growth, and lead your family to grow spiritually as well. Ask God's Holy Spirit to lead you every day.

- **H**ave a renewal of your faith. Here is a Guarantee for Christians: if you will invest yourself in a more intimate and closer relationship with the Lord, he will bring blessings into every area of your life that honors him.

May God bless you with great success as you consider these truths and Layoff Proof Your Job and Layoff Proof Yourself!

# Addendum

Following are a few of my favorite Christian websites.

www.biblegateway.com
www.christianretirement.com
www.christiansunited.com
www.focusonthefamily.com
www.gty.org
www.intouch.org
www.oneplace.com
www.rbc.org
www.samaritanspurse.org